THE TIES THAT BIND,
ANTIQUE DOLL COSTUMES, 1820–1910

FLORENCE THERIAULT

Gold Horse Publishing

© Copyright 2009 Theriault's Gold Horse Publishing. All rights reserved.

No part of this book may be reproduced or utilized in any form or by any means, electronic or mechanical, including photocopying, recording, or by an information retrieval system, without permission, in writing, from the author or the publisher.

To order additional copies contact:
Dollmasters, PO Box 2319, Annapolis, MD 21404
Tel. 800-966-3655   Fax 410-571-9605
www.dollmasters.com

Design: Travis Hammond
Photography: Gerald Nelson

$49
ISBN: 1-931503-56-7
Printed in Hong Kong

This antique doll costume collection auctioned by Theriault's of Annapolis, Maryland, January 11, 2009.

www.theriaults.com.

The stitches that weave our costumes, or those of our dolls, are also the ties that bind our memories to past pleasant times. Words can somehow not capture the exact color blue – was it azure, or aqua, or the color of sky? – that a certain doll was wearing on the day we saw her in the window. Just how did the skirt drape with an elusive yet perfectly structured shape? It seemed so simple, yet what were the hidden secrets of construction that created that look? And the bonnet that framed her little face like the gilded wooden frame of a fine painting, or the shoes so intricately constructed that they fit her feet like skin, yet still were possible to remove. It is true that the face of the doll first draws us to her, yet it is also certain that clothes do make the doll. ⚜

1. Fine Early High-Waist Gown

4" shoulders. 16" overall length. Of a very finely woven cotton/silk with lustrous finish, the high-waisted gown designed for early lady doll features shirring at the bodice with a border of hand-made looped braid, above a full-length skirt with flat-front and cartridge-pleated back, both neckline and waist secured with strings en coulisse for adjustable fit. The pouf sleeves are artfully-constructed with shirring that is given added emphasis with intermittent gathering threads. Circa 1820. $900/1200

2. Patterned Rose Silk Gown for Early Lady Doll

3" shoulders. 6" waist. 12" overall length. Of a very fine rose patterned silk faille, the cut of the petite gown is low on the shoulders, yet with a modestly cut V-shaped bodice with dart-shaped snug fit and having piping at the darts and waist. The very wide collar is triple-pleated and extends in points over the very full lantern sleeves with tulle ruffle at the bands. The skirt is pleated all around, meeting at the center front. Some fraility to silk. Circa 1840. $500/700

3. Fine Early Brown Silk Gown with Embroidered Gold Metallic Panel, and Slippers

6" shoulders. 8" waist. 22" overall floor length. The finely woven brown silk gown features a rounded neckline with strings en coulisse for adjustable fit, fitted bodice with shaping darts at the back, self-cording at the waist above a cartridge-pleated skirt, sleeves that are pleated at the shoulders and widen to the turned sleeve edges. The bodice is lined with fine muslin, and there is a detachable panel of gold silk that extends down the entire front and is encrusted with superb gold metallic threads and paillettes. A matching embroidery detail appears on the wide sleeve cuffs and on the side and back panel of the skirt, and there is a metallic border on the skirt. Included are matching pair of silk faille slippers with metallic embroidery. Late 18th century. $800/1200

4. Early Plum Silk Gown with Pouf Sleeves
4" shoulder width. 7" waist. 13" overall. Of a fine crisp purple/plum silk, the gown features a low-rounded neckline above a dart-shaped bodice and tiny waist. The skirt with all-around pleats is very full and given added shape by an unusual self-piping at the bottom of the hem. The sleeves are an extravagant pouf formed by pleats at the shoulders and cuffs, and hold their shape by an internal straight-cut sleeve lining. The dress is fully muslin-lined, hand-stitched, and has hook and eye closure. Circa 1830. $600/900

5. Lady's Black Taffeta Gown with Pouf Sleeves
4" shoulder width. 8" waist. 15" overall length. Of black silk and having rounded neckline with full bodice and flat-front skirt, the gown features wide pouf sleeves with full-cut lining. There is a patterned cotton lining on the bodice, and hook and eye closures. The somewhat irregular fit and awkward construction suggest workmanship by a child. 19th century, era uncertain. $200/300

6. Miniature Early Gown for Lady Doll
1 3/4" shoulder width. 3" waist. 6" overall length. Of soft silk/wool in a rich muted purple color, the gown features a rounded neckline with pleated collar that extends to sleeve tops, dart-shaped bodice, set-in waistband, full skirt, beautifully shaped sleeves that are very full at the upper arms, and curve gracefully to the wrist. Fine old cotton lining. Circa 1830. $400/500

7. Fine Muslin Gown with Woven Dots

6" shoulders. 11" waist. 5"l. to waist. 21" overall length. Of a very delicate loosely woven sheer muslin that is enhanced with interwoven large dots, the gown has a low-rounded neckline with handmade lace edging that matches the wrist lace. The long sleeves have narrow pleats at the shoulders and are poufed twice at the upper arms to create a rich fullness. The bodice is full at the front with flat-cut lining that gives form, and dart-shaped at the lined back. Tiny gathers form the extended-length skirt which is designed for easy alteration of the hem. there is very narrow self-piping at the neckline and waist. Circa 1850. $400/600

8. Fine Muslin Gown with Woven Dots with Early Woven Bonnet

6" shoulders. 12" waist. 18" overall length. A superb gown of very fine sheer muslin with thick interwoven dots has a low-rounded neckline with lace ruffle, a full gathered bodice that extends over the shoulders gains its shape from a fitted interior bodice, is edged with lace, and forms into a 3" band of tightly shirred waistband. The pagoda-shaped sleeves have lace edging, and the skirt has cartridge pleating all-around. Included is a tightly-woven straw bonnet with rose silk borders edged with delicate silk fringe. Circa 1840. $600/900

9. Exceptional Child's Floor-Length Gown with Elaborate Ruffles and lace

8" shoulders. 19" waist. 32" overall length. Of a beautifully woven jaconet with defined checkerboard and dot pattern, the slightly-high-waisted gown features a V-shaped confection of ruffled lace and muslin on the bodice that is repeated in a larger scale on the cartridge-pleated long skirt. The widely poufed sleeves gain their shape from a fitted under-sleeve and are lace-edged. A child's costume intended for a gala, the gown is easily adaptable to a large bébé, its low neckline especially pleasing on a model with bisque shoulder plate, such as Bébé Bru. Circa 1875. $700/1000

10. Early Coiffe with Pont d'Esprit Lace and Aqua Silk Trim

5" inside head with. A seven-piece inner construction of heavy card-paper (visible inside the bonnet, and possibly originally lined to hide the construction detail) is stitched together to give shape to the bonnet which sits at the back of the head and is designed to allow for chignon. The coiffe is richly decorated with superb early pont d'esprit and Alencon lace with a tightly pleated medallion-like effect at the back. A wide aqua ribbon is pleated to form a banding around the cap and forms a wide bow with streamers that fall onto the nape. The coiffe is ink-inscribed Henriette Pullaird inside. Circa 1840. $300/500

11. Fine Muslin Gown with Interwoven Dots and Printed Blue Flowers

7" shoulders. 13" waist. 17" overall. A delicate summery-weight white muslin fabric is enhanced by with tiny interwoven dots and tiny blue flowers and leaves, lending style to the simple two-piece gown with dropped shoulders, strings en coulisse waist, tatted lace on the neckline and cuffs of long sleeves, and having a flat-panel front skirt with cartridge-pleated back. Circa 1870. $400/500

12. Early Two-Piece Gown of White Mull with Fitted Jacket and Demi-Train

6" shoulders. 8" waist. 12" front skirt. Of very fine cotton mull, the delicate white gown with abstract four-color triangle shapes, features a dart-shaped basque jacket that arches gracefully over the hips, is elongated at the front, has ox-pleated tails at the back, and long coat sleeves. The matching skirt has a ruffled hem and extends 2" longer at the back in a demi-train. Circa 1850. $400/600

13. The Silk "Bird Bonnet" with Lace and Woven Straw Decorations, Paris Label

5" inside diameter. The firmly-shaped flat-top bonnet attains a soft rounded shape with draped and folded ivory silk fabric that is overlaid with a wide silk band edged with embroidered tulle, The upturned small brim has a band of straw braid, and a wide loop-pattern straw braid surrounds the bonnet edge. Perched atop the bonnet is a delightful bird, woven and shaped of fine straw with "feathered" details. A paper label inside the muslin lining features a lion and unicorn medallion and "Paris" in gilt lettering. Circa 1850. $400/500

14. Cotton Print Dress with Neatly Shaped Sleeves

4" shoulders. 8" adjustable waist. 18" overall. A fine cotton with delicate abstract print in mauve and coral, features strings en coulisse at both neckline and waist for adjustable fit, fully lined bodice, pagoda-shaped sleeves with a gathered ruffle above the fitted cuff, eyelet edging on the cuff, neckline lace. A simple yet beautiful dress that works well on early child dolls, or on early paper-mache or china doll, with adjustable fit. Circa 1860. $300/500

15. Early Cotton Print Dress with Pagoda Sleeves

4" shoulder width. 8" waist. 12" overall length. Of dainty white cotton with abstract rose-shaded pattern, the gown features a slightly-rounded neckline, full bodice that gains its shape with a 1" band of ruching at the center waist, set-in waistband, and three-tiered full skirt. The pagoda-style sleeves are trimmed with two wide self-ruffles, and self-cording details at the shoulders lends a fine finished look. Circa 1860. $400/500

16. Exceptional Thickly-Quilted Early Bonnet with Very Wide Brim

5" inside head diameter. 5"l. 5" width of brim all-around the face. Of a cotton twill with mauve transfer-printed abstract circular design, the bonnet has nankeen lining and is thickly quilted. Although the quilting is, presumably, for warmth, it also gives a firm structure to the bonnet. The very wide brim extends 5" all-around the face with cotton ties at the neck, and at the neck points of the brim. Circa 1840. $200/400

17. Woven Bourrelet Cap with Rose Satin Bow

5" head width. A firm-sided tightly-woven straw cap with open zig-zag weave about the upper edge is designed to cover a toddler's head and protect it from tumbles, has brown cord decorations, sienna cloth edging, and a coral satin bow. Circa 1860. $300/400

18. Miniature Woven Straw Bourrelet

1.5" (4 cm.) A firm-sided hat of horizontally-woven straw has rounded cap top, and brown-silk edging along with richly-arranged brown silk bows at the crown. The hat was designed to fit snugly onto a baby's head to protect the baby during a tumble. Circa 1850. $300/500

19. Cotton Day Gown with Feather-Stitch Detail

5" shoulders. 9" waist. 23" overall length. 5" to waist. A cotton day gown in very narrow red and cream stripes has square-cut neckline above a cartridge-pleated full bodice, wide set-in waist band, and long flowing skirt with cartridge pleating, open front, and edged with a self-ruffle. The pagoda-shaped sleeves have a self-band and self-ruffle with lace and cotton sous-sleeves, and there is brown feather-stitching on the neckline, sleeves and waist. Circa 1860. $300/500

20. Fine White Voile Gown with Patterned Flowers and Embroidered Collar
6" shoulder width. 11" waist. 23" overall. The lady-doll costume features a full gathered bodice with pearl button closure, very full sleeves with defined cuffs, and and a five-tiered skirt, each tier resting upon a tulle liner,. The gown is edged in lace at each tier and a fine embroidered detachable collar is at the neckline. Handmade costume for large slender-bodied lady doll. Circa 1875. $300/500

21. White Dimity Gown with Exceptional Needlework
4" shoulder width. 26"l. Of dainty white cotton dimity, the low-bodice gown with little cap sleeves features a high waist with string en coulisse for adjustable fit, an attached yoke of fine dotted Swiss batiste with lace edging that extends the entire length of the gown, embroidered daisies at the skirt, along with original underslip. Although a baby doll dress, the unusual two-tier skirt level would allow an easy adjustment for use as gown for child or lady doll. Circa 1850. $300/500

22. FINE WHITE SHEER MUSLIN GOWN WITH UNDERGARMENT AND JACKET

6" shoulders. 12" waist. 18" overall length. Of finely woven sheer muslin the white gown features a rounded neckline, short capelet sleeves, and a V-shaped waist that is formed from tightly shirred detail at the lower bodice. The cartridge-pleated full skirt is enhanced with six bands of self-fabric. Included is a matching full slip, and an delicately woven "petit pois" muslin sacque with pagoda-shaped sleeves and handmade lace edging. Circa 1850. $400/600

23. SHEER MUSLIN GOWN WITH MAUVE DIAMOND PRINT AND RIBBONS

4 1/2" shoulder width. 9" waist. 14" overall length. A fine quality woven sheer muslin with lattice design and transfer-printed mauve diamond designs, has low rounded neckline that is edged with purple ribbon and handmade lace, and pagoda-shaped sleeves with three rows of trim. The set-in waistband has a lace overlay, and the skirt is cartridge-pleated. Circa 1860. $400/500.

24. DELICATE WHITE COTTON BLOUSE

4" shoulders. 5" length. Of finely woven white cotton, the blouse has strings en coulisse at both neckline and waist for adjustable fit, and is decorated with a V-shaped panel that extends below the waist and is embroidered with Brittany-style designs. The panel is scallop-edged and the capelet sleeves over the full-length sous-sleeves are also scallop-edged and embroidered. Circa 1850. $200/300

25. Blue Cotton Print Gown with Tiered Ruffles at Sides and Back
3 1/2" shoulders. 7" waist. 11" overall length. A tightly-woven cotton in very narrow stripes of alternating dark and light blue and white stripes features a lace-trimmed square-cut neckline, fitted bodice, flat-front skirt with curved appliques of same fabric, and four-tiers of ruffles that begin at the sides and extend all-around the back. Circa 1860. $200/400

26. Blue Cotton Dress for Slender Early Lady Doll
4 1/2" shoulder width. 9" waist. 19" overall length. Of a finely woven cotton with minute woven pattern, the gown has a slightly rounded neckline with V-point that matches the V-shape of the set-in waist. the gown has long fitted sleeves with hooks and eyes at the wrists, and a cartridge pleated full skirt. Self-cording decorates the center bodice, neckline waist, shoulder edges, and wrists. Circa 1840. $300/500

27. Cream and Aqua Gown with Blue Silk Trim
3 1/2" shoulder width. 8" waist. 11" overall length. Of a fine silk/wool twill, in a striped cream and aqua woven pattern, the gown has a rounded neckline, short fitted sleeves, dart-shaped torso at the front, set-in waist at the back above box pleats that form into an elongated skirt length at the back. The gown is decorated with an aqua banding and lace at the neckline, white buttons and hand-made buttonholes at the front, and a sky blue silk pocket and sash loops at the side, and is fully-lined. Circa 1860. $400/500

28. WHITE COTTON SHIFT AND GARMENTS

5" shoulders. 10" waist. 15" length. A tightly woven cotton night shift has hand-made cut-work edging on collar, cuffs and detachable belt. Also included is fitted blouse with flared hips, drawstring petticoat, and a night-shirt with tucking at the front, set-in cuffs and collar, and tiny pearl buttons. Circa 1865. $200/300

29. UNUSUAL COTTON DAY DRESS WITH ASIAN INFLUENCE

3 1/2" shoulder width. 15" length. A crisp cotton print with narrow diagonal stripes and white bands is used for this striking day dress with orange and brown braid frog closures and white pearl buttons on the front opening. The braid trim is repeated around the neckline, sleeves, edges of two pockets, and at the back waist above a box-pleat that extends into demi-train. The pagoda-shaped sleeves enhance the overall Asian influence of the costume. A ruffle of tulle is at the neckline. Circa 1865. $300/500

30. WHITE PIQUE BAVOLET BONNET WITH LOOP-DE-LOOP SOUTACHE DESIGN

5" inside head width. 12" overall length. Of narrow-ribbed white pique, the bonnet has a 2 1/2" folded-over brim extended 6" bavolet below the fitted cap-back and is decorated with an imaginative soutache embroidery in a series of interconnecting loops. Circa 1850. $200/300

31. WHITE PIQUE BAVOLET BONNET FOR CHILD, WITH SOUTACHE TRIM
5" facial width. 12" overall length. The ribbed white pique bonnet, with fleecy liner for warmth, has a generous 5" fold-over brim around the entire face, and extended bavolet given shape by box pleats. The cap is generously embroidered with white soutache, and the cap is secured by hidden ties. A child's garment that is suitable for a larger doll. Circa 1850. $200/300

32. WHITE PIQUE BEST BONNET WITH CROWN FURBELOWS
5" inside head width. 10" overall including bavolet. Of white pique, the bonnet features a triple-wire brim with gathers and cording, sourmounted by a crown of soutache-edged furbelows. The soutache embroidery contines around the crown, generously covered with double-box-pleated bavolet and forms an elaborate floral and geometric design at the back of head. Circa 1850. $300/500

33. WHITE PIQUE SKIRT WITH BLACK SOUTACHE
7" waist. 7" skirt length. 10" overall. Of horizontally-arranged finely-ribbed white pique, the skirt features a fitted high bodice with three-button closure at the back, above a flared skirt with double-box pleats all around. The skirt is decorated with black soutache and white braid in a zig-zag manner, and the trim continues on the bodice with an underlay of ecru woven fabric. Circa 1860. $300/400

34. WHITE PIQUE ENSEMBLE WITH PAGODA SLEEVES AND SOUTACHE TRIM
5" shoulder width. 7" skirt length. Of horizontally ribbed white pique, comprising a fitted hip-length

jacket has self-covered buttons, and rich soutache and applique braid trim. Along with a matching box-pleated skirt. The ensemble is a slender cut, unusual for costumes of this era. Circa 1860. $200/400

35. French Bonnet "A Deux Bonjours" and Cashmere Cape

Bonnet 5" l., 2" inside head diameter. 8"l. cape. An elaborately woven bonnet with upturned brim at front and back has red silk lining, black velvet banding and streamers, and an elaborate soutache braid of woven rattan; along with fine black cashmere cape with black silk lining, elaborate black silk soutache embroidery, black lace edging, and internal hidden ties for shape. Circa 1850. $300/500

36. Blue Wool Serge Jacket with Soutache

7" shoulder width. 7" overall length. Of fine wool serge in a rich sky blue, the jacket is fully-lined with a polished blue sateen, and is richly embroidered with a cream soutache on the 4" box-pleated collar and sleeve edges. Circa 1850. $300/500

37. Cotton Twill Bonnet with Embroidery Pattern

1 3/4" inside head width. The white cotton twill with crisp original sizing is formed into a bonnet with box-pleated face ruffle, lappets, and self-fabric bow at the crown and nape. The fabric is printed with a blue embroidery pattern in soutache style, designed as a pattern for young needle-worker learning the technique. Circa 1865. $200/300

38. Two Pairs of Early Cobbled Footwear

Comprising 3 1/4" black leather boots with laced front, and having thick hand-cobbled leather soles with defined heels. And 3 1/2" thick leather slippers with thong ties and hammered leather soles. Circa 1850. $200/300

39. Fine Sheer Cotton Dress with Rose Floral Print

7" shoulder width. 18" waist. 23" overall length. A child's costume suitable for costuming larger doll, is of very delicate cotton with faintly printed narrow rose and cream stripes and a patterned rose-petal design. The rounded neckline and pouf sleeves have strings en coulisse for adjustable fit, and there is a 1" band of ruching above the set-in waistband. The full gathered skirt gains shape from the very narrow cartridge pleats just below the waist band. Circa 1860. $300/500

40. Woven Straw Bonnet with Elaborate Silk Ribbons, and Woven Slippers

5" inside width. Designed to perch on the crown of the head, the tightly-woven cap is nearly-flat-topped and has a 1" brim all-around that is richly decorated with ivory silk taffeta streamers and banding. Along with 5 1/2"l. pair of woven straw slippers with decorative red silk lining and bows, the bows centered by tiny woven straw balls. Circa 1860. $400/500

41. Finely Woven Bonnet with Rose Silk Lining

6" inside head width. The bonnet

is woven in an intricate style with tight bands alternating with open-looped designs that allows the rose silk color of the lining to show. Other intricate loops and braids decorate the back and sides. The inside of the wide face brim is lined with shirred rose silk. Circa 1860. $300/400

42. BLUE AND WHITE COTTON PLAID GOWN WITH PAGODA SLEEVES
5 1/2" shoulder width. 12" waist. 19" overall length. A fine cotton gown in a fine plaid of multi-shade blue and white with narrow red striping for color accent, has sloping shoulders, V-shaped neckline with stitched on cotton lace collar, pagoda-shaped sleeves, and a dart-shaped bodice with over-stitching detail. The defined waist has self-cording edge above a cartridge-pleated skirt. Circa 1850. $400/500

43. ROYAL PURPLE CASHMERE GOWN WITH BELLOWS POCKET AND HANDKERCHIEF
5" shoulder width. 11" relaxed waist. 15" overall length. Of a finely woven silk/cashmere wool purple fabric with interwoven black Z-design, the rounded neckline dress has front and back dart-shaping, hook and eye closures down the entire front with purple covered decorative buttons. The pouf sleeves gain their shape from a straight-sided liner and there is lace edging at the neckline, sleeve bands, and above and below the stitched-down pleated border at the hem. A side-hip pocket is lace-edged and has a lace-edged hankie, and the skirt back is slightly elongated at the back for an elegant look. Circa 1875. $400/600

44. FINE WHITE COTTON DRESS WITH EMBROIDERED BODICE PANEL
6" shoulder width. 13" waist. 16" overall length. A polished white cotton dress with rounded neckline, sloping shoulders with set-in full sleeves having three bands of scalloped-edge embroidery at the top of the sleeve and a wide embroidered cuff, has strings en coulisse for adjustable fit at the neckline. A wide V-shaped panel with attached bretelles covers the entire bodice with exceptional embroidery, and, above the cartridge-pleated skirt, there is a set-in waist band whose embroidered details are repeated in the insert skirt band and scalloped edge hem. Circa 1875. $300/500

45. FINE SHEER MUSLIN GOWN WITH ATTACHED UNDER-SLIP
4" shoulders. 7 1/2" waist. 13" overall length. Of finely woven sheer muslin, the gown features a slightly high waist,, elbow-length sleeves and a daintily gathered skirt with two tiers of ruffles at the hemline that are captured in a scalloped-edge effect, with coral silk decorative bows at sleeves, bodice and skirt, lace edging and an attached under-slip for the skirt with ruffled hem. Circa 1850. $300/500

46. Superb Brown Linsey-Woolsey Gown with Black Silk Apron

6" shoulder width. 13" waist. 18" overall length. A very crisp and sturdy chestnut brown gown of linsey-woolsey features a front close below V-shaped rounded neckline, and neatly-shaped sleeves with black velvet inner edge. With the gown is a black silk apron with silk-velvet edging, silk pockets with wide tatted edging that matches the tatting on the apron bib. A finely woven black lace fichu extends around the neckline and is tucked under the apron bib. Circa 1860. $600/900

47. Small Brown and Cream Plaid Linsey-Woolsey Dress

2 1/2" shoulders. 5" waist. 7" overall length. A richly patterned linsey-woolsey dress in shades of brown, grey and cream, has a fitted yoke above an all-around box-pleated bodice, upturned cuffs, loosely-fitted waist, and a flat-front skirt with box-pleats at the sides and back. Three white buttons with loop closures are at the back. Circa 1860s. $300/400

48. Red Plaid Linsey-Woolsey Dress with Black Velvet Ribbons

3 1/2" shoulder width. 7" waist. 13" overall length. A red plaid one-piece dress of linsey-woolsey has a self collar, coat-shaped sleeves, fitted fotice and waist, and gathered skirt with extra tier at the hemline that is barely visible but gives shape to the skirt. There are three bands of narrow black velvet ribbon at the bodice and cuffs, and three black buttons with loop closure at the back. Circa 1860s. $300/400

49. Blue and White Linsey-Woolsey Dress with Bellows Pockets

3 1/2" shoulder width 13" overall. In a vibrant plaid of dark and light blue with cream, the one piece gown gains shape from fitted darts at the back and tapered sides. It has seven front buttons with hand-made button holes, coat sleeves, inside front lining, slightly extended

length at the back, and a pair of small bellow-shaped pockets at the front. Circa 1860s. $400/500

50. Early Silver Cap with Silver Metallic Embroidery

5" inside width. The cap, designed to closely fit the head, has a hand-stitched homespun inner lining, stiffened silver fabric cover, and is richly decorated with silver metallic embroidery around the edges and in six rays emanating from a center "sun" at the back center of the head. The "sun" is accented with a silver thread tassel. Early 19th century. $300/400

51. Brown and Black Silk Satin Gown with White Beading

3" shoulder width. 7" waist. 13" overall length. A soft silk dress with fitted black bodice and brown flat-front skirt has 3/4 sleeves with black outer side and brown inner side, and is decorated with applique white beads and a row of coral silk bows. Circa 1875. $300/500

51.1. Black Silk Beaded Tunic with Fine Dimity Blouse

4 1/2" shoulder width. 8" length. A black silk faille tunic with waist, flared hips and open front is trimmed with black beads and entirely edged with black lace. Below is a very fine dimity cotton blouse with coat sleeves and dainty embroidery and lace at the neckline and cuffs. Circa 1865. $400/600

52. Fine Three-Piece Ensemble for Early Poupée

4" shoulder width. 8" waist. 12" overall. Comprising a jacket and over-skirt of bengaline silk with delicately interwoven grey stripes on a cream background; and an underskirt of grey and coral silk. Both jacket and underskirt have van-dyke edging along the bottom edges, epaulets and faux-pocket flaps are trimmed in a narrow coral silk to match the skirt. Handmade coral-stitched buttonholes nicely contrast with the brass buttons with raised designs. The unfitted jacket front curves nicely at the sides and has loose dart-shaping at the back. The lustrous grey silk skirt has vertical coral piping and is edged with a wide band of coral silk. The workmanship is couturiere quality. Circa 1860. $1200/1500

53. Brown and Cream Woven Cotton/Silk Two-Piece Ensemble

4" shoulders. 6" waist. 10" skirt. A brown cotton jacket with flared sides, dropped shoulders, and cost sleeves is trimmed with the skirt fabric in box-pleats that form around the jacket edge and neck.; there is silk braid on the cuffs. The skirt has cartridge pleating at sides and back, and a flat front, three ruffle tiers at the bottom skirt (lined for shape) edged by silk braid. Circa 1860. $700/900

55 back.

53, 54, 55.

54. Bronze-Green Silk Ensemble for Larger Poupée
5" shoulder width. 10" waist. 18" overall length. Of bronze-green silk, the two-piece ensemble features a box-shaped jacket with long coat sleeves, and a flat-front skirt with elongated back skirt. Both jacket and skirt are trimmed with edging of pale green and cream with black lace edging, faux-pockets, and lace edging at the cuffs. Circa 1860. $600/900

55. Petite Bengaline Silk Gown for Petite Poupée
2" shoulder width. 4" waist. 7" overall length. Natural color bengaline silk gown is constructed as one-piece although appearing to be a three-piece ensemble. The fitted bodice has two diamond-point shapes below the waist, 3/4 sleeves and an elaborate flounce at the back. The flat-front skirt has a three-tiered arrangement at the hem including scalloped layer, and the arrangement is enhanced at the back with full gathers. A bronze-green rick-rack decorates the gown, with a delicate lace border at the neckline. Circa 1860. $700/900

56. MAUVE AND CREAM SILK GOWN
4" shoulder width. 8" waist. 11" overall length. Of a delicate shadow pane design in mauve and cream silk, the one-piece gown features a rounded neckline, pouf sleeves with sleeve-bands, wide bretelles that virtually hide the sleeves, fitted bodice and a very full tightly-gathered skirt. The gown is decorated in a simple yet elegant manner with looped mauve silk cording arranged in irregular lengths. Circa 1860. $800/1000

57. BURGUNDY SILK ENSEMBLE FOR SLENDER TALL DOLL
2 1/2" shoulder width. 6" waist. 11" overall. Of burgundy silk, comprising long skirt with three rows of self cording, white chemisette, and a burgundy bolero jacket with large pouf sleeves trimmed with three rows of cording. In the 1850 manner, age uncertain. $200/400

58. IVORY SILK SATIN BAVOLET BONNET WITH SILK FRINGE
4" inside head width. Of lined silk satin with luxurious finish, the bonnet features a very extended length bavolet edged in elongated silk fringe. A double row of fine lace encircles the face, disguising the wire under-

frame that gives shape to the bonnet, and a large ivory silk bow is at the crest. Circa 1875. $300/500

59. Two Demi-Train Petticoats and an Over-skirt

7"-8" waists. Comprising a pont d'esprit over-skirt, rose tulle back lining, gathered side flounces and decorated with rose satin bows, along with two petticoats with rich garniture and trim, each having extended back length for wear with demi-train gowns. $200/400

60. Ivory Tartalane Gown with Torchon Lace Edging

3" shoulder width. 6" waist. 10" overall length. A crisp natural silk gown is completely overlaid with tartalane creating an airy, delicate appearance, with dart-shaped bodice that appears to be separate but is actually attached to the skirt. The bodice features a rounded neckline and pouf sleeves. The skirt front is flat-panelled although the full tartalane overlay created a gathered look, and the back is very generously shaped with bustled tartalane and demi-train. A creamy torchon lace edging is around the collar, sleeves, and bottom edge of bodice and tartalane, and ivory satin bows and tiny rosebuds add decorative touches. Circa 1865. $500/700

60.

61. Cream Silk Gown with Aqua Silk Trim

3 1/2" shoulder length. 7" waist. 10" overall. Cream silk faille two-piece gown with dart-shaped bodice, and square-cut neckline, along with a flat-front skirt that flares at the sides and forms into gathers a the back. The gown is trimmed with aqua silk faille surrounded in elaborately constructed bands at the bottom of the bodice, sleeves and hem. Beneath each band of aqua faille trim is a wide border of pont d'argentan lace. Circa 1865. $600/800

62. Superb Ivory Silk Satin Bonnet and Satin Shoes

5" inside head width. 7" length shoes. The bonnet back is embroidered with a golden soutache emblem and has a box-pleated bavolet with silk fringe edging. The crown is an extravaganza of decoration with four layers of various laces and trims, presented in graduated width with a culminating confection at the peak dotted with a silk ribbon frou-frou. The bonnet is muslin lined and padded, and has ivory silk streamers. The ivory silk satin slippers have hand-stitched interiors, an ivory bow trim, and soft kid-skin soles and heels. Circa 1880. $500/800

63. Green Wool Serge Hooded Coat for Lady Doll

4" shoulders. 15" overall length. Fine bronze-green wool serge coat features flared side, flat front, single box pleat at the back, self-covered buttons and hand-made button holes, coat sleeves, over-sized pockets, and a hood with adjustable drawstring and having black fabric lining at the inside edge. Circa 1865. $300/400

64. Peach Silk Bonnet with Dainty Flowers

2 1/2" head width. Designed to perch atop the head, the firm-shaped bonnet of peach silk has a lavishly draped border with long streamers; the fabric-edging is a finishing scallop-cut, and the bonnet is trimmed with a monture of tiny wild-flowers. Lined. Circa 1870. $300/500

65. Patterned White Pique Two Piece Ensemble

3 1/2" shoulder width. 8" waist. 10" jacket length. 15" overall length. Of fine horizontally ribbed white pique with transfer print of tiny red flowers, the two-piece gown comprises a fitted basque jacket with wide flaring hips that extend 3/4 of the skirt length, having six wooden buttons over hook and eye, long pagoda sleeves, white braid edging on jacket, collar and cuffs. With tightly-gathered full-length skirt. Circa 1860. $500/800

66. Navy Blue and Black Striped Two-Piece Silk Ensemble for Lady Doll

4" shoulder width. 9" waist. 15" overall. Of a crisp silk in blue and black narrow stripes, the two-piece gown features a jacket with fitted yoke above a pleated bodice, black button front with hand-made button holes, long fitted sleeves and blue edged black velvet ribbon banding. The flat-front long skirt has pleated back and muslin dust ruffle with lace edging. Circa 1870. $500/700

67. Purple Silk And Woolen Two-Piece Suit for Lady doll

4" shoulder width. 7" waist. 14" overall length. The two-piece ensemble features a neatly-fitted basque jacket that fits snugly over the hips and flounces slightly at the back, and having a hand-made trim of purple zig-zag over white narrow lace border. There is lace edging at the neckline, yoke and cuffs. The skirt is of rich purple silk satin with flat-panel front and pleated back, and is edged at the hem with a lace-edged pleated dust ruffle. Circa 1865. $500/800

68. Black Velvet and Purple Silk Gown for Lady Doll

4" shoulder width. 8" waist. 12" overall length. Made of a very luxurious fabric of alternating narrow stripes of black velvet and purple silk, the one piece gown features a fitted bodice with dart-shaped back, set-in long sleeves with box-pleated purple silk trim with black velvet edging at the shoulders that is repeated at the cuffs and at the bottom hem line. The waist has a fitted black velvet belt and purple silk ribbons, and the gored back skirt has a demi-train. There is some fraility and fading of the purple silk. Circa 1865. $400/500

69. White Waffle-Weave Pique Two-Piece Dress with Red Piping

Of crisp pique in a waffle-weave pattern, the dress features a fitted bodice with very wide V-shaped collar, box-pleated flared short sleeves, and wide flare below the waist. The skirt has box pleats at the front, and narrow-gathered skirt. Red twill piping edge the sleeves, collar and bodice hem. Circa 1860. $600/800

70. Cream Cashmere Hood with Red Silk Ruffle

2" face width. 6" overall. Of soft cream cashmere with painted dots, quilted silk lining, the snood-shaped hood has capelet collar and is edged in narrow red silk ribbon that forms a cluster of ruffles at the crown. A few minor moth holes. Circa 1865. $200/300

71. Cream Cotton Three-Piece Fashion Gown for Lady Doll

4 1/2" shoulder width. 10" waist. 15" overall length. Of fine creamy color with interwoven fabric design, the gown features a blouse with pleated bodice, and long coat sleeves with sewn-on wide pleated and lace-edged cuffs; an under-skirt with fullness at the back and a pleated dust ruffle; and an elaborately constructed over-skirt with shirring detail at front and sides, and created a voluminous back bustle. There is lace edging at the bottom edge of the over-skirt and at the neckline. Circa 1870. $600/900

73 detail.

72 detail.

72, 73.

72. Lustrous Cotton Day Dress with Demi-Train

4" shoulder width. 12" overall length. Made of a very fine white cotton fabric with alternating shadow stripe of polished cotton, the flat-front day gown has six pearl buttons and hand-made button holes at the front centered by panels of fine Argentan lace that extend over the shoulders to form a lace frame at the dart-shaped back. The lace trim is repeated as a jabot and at the cuffs, and there is a scalloped lace edging at the hem which, at the back, has a double-box-pleat demi-train at the center. Circa 1870 $400/500

73. White Cotton Sateen Lady Gown

5" shoulder width. 10" waist. 17" overall length. The one-piece fitted gown of fine lustrous cotton with woven design features dart-shaping at front and back, set-in hidden waist, dart-shaped fullness at the back hips, coat sleeves with wide cuffs, nine pearl buttons with hand-made button holes, and a band of alternating wide and narrow pleats at the hem framed by a row of cotton torchon lace. Circa 1870. $400/600

74.

74. Brown Velvet Bonnet with Rosebud Crown

2 1/2" inside width. The brown velvet cap, designed to form to the back of the head, is firm-structured, edged at the back with narrow shaded rose silk ribbons and having a black lace bavolet. A 2" high stiffened woven crown rises above the cap and provides a background for a cluster of silk roses and leaves. Circa 1870. $300/500

75. Cream Ball Gown with Extended Train
3 1/2" shoulder width. 8" Waist. 13" front overall length. 23" back skirt train. Made of fine silvery-cream opaque mousseline with interwoven blue flowers, the gown features a low rounded neckline, fitted bodice with front hook and eye closure, short pouf sleeves, flat-front flared skirt with self-ruffle at the

hemline and a very extended train. The gown is decorated with teal-blue lappets that are edged with metallic-silver braid and dotted with white buttons. The trim is repeated around the neckline, sleeves and waist that is accented with a large teal-blue silk ribbon rosette. Circa 1865. $900/1100

76. Pale-Golden Silk Gown with Demi-Train

4" shoulder width. 11" overall length. A one-piece gown of very luxurious soft silk satin in a rich buttery-gold color has flat-front, flared sides, and dart shaped back with box-pleat at the back waist that forms into a demi-train. The rounded neck-line, angled front closure with hook and eye, pouf sleeves and hem are edged with embroidered tulle and there are two ivory satin bows at the front. Circa 1870. $300/400

77. Ivory Pongee Silk Gown for Lady Doll

4 1/2" shoulder width. 10" waist. 18" overall length. A creamy ivory one-piece gown of pongee silk has dart-shaping, fitting snugly over the hips, v-shaped neckline, 3/4 sleeves with lace edging, and an attached over-skirt below the hips that reaches to a wide self-ruffle at the hem. There is a box-pleated demi-train with muslin lining. The gown is trimmed with blue and ivory applique silk ribbons, and there are six pearl buttons and hand-made button-holes at the front. Circa 1875. $500/800

78. Aqua Silk Gown with Matching Bonnet

4" shoulder width. 12" length. A turquoise silk gown achieves its shape from darts at the back, double box-pleat below the waist. The gown has a simple rounded neckline and elbow-length sleeves that are edged in lace and there is a wide ruffle of lace that extends down the entire front of the gown and edges the bottom hem.

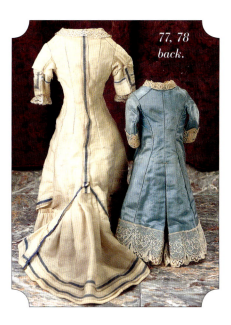

77, 78 back.

Included is a matching silk faille bonnet with ivory streamers. Circa 1875. $700/900

79. White Pique Day Dress and Lace Coiffe

4" shoulder width. 12" overall length. 2 1/2" inside lace coiffe head width. The gown, of horizontally-ribbed white pique has flared sides with flat-front, and a center box pleat at the back with two smaller pleats also at the back from collar to hem giving a fullness to the gown. The modified coat sleeves with flared cuffs and the entire button-front and hem-line are scallop-shaped and edged with thick overcast stitching. There are pearl buttons and hand-made button-holes and the collar is dainty embroidered cut-work known as broderie anglaise. Along with a lace and silk coiffe that captures the hair and frames the face with a padded lace-covered cap, large ivory faille bow, and lace ruffle (stain on one corner of bow). Circa 1865. $500/800

80. Cream Jacket with Blue Buttons and Braid

4" should width. A jacket of very delicate wool/cotton is accented with tiny blue woven dots, has hook and eye closure under blue silk-covered buttons, and braid trim at neckline, edging, cuffs, along with epaulets at both front and back shoulders. Circa 1865. $200/300

81. White Mull Sacque with Delicate Ruffles

4" shoulder width. 7" overall length. A very fine mull fabric composes a sacque with slightly flared sides, coat sleeves with narrow wrists, and a gracefully curved edge that is decorated with a self-ruffle that is repeated at the yoke. Circa 1865. $200/300

82. WHITE PIQUE DRESS FOR LADY DOLL WITH ELABORATE HAND-MADE ZIG-ZAG TRIM

4" shoulder width. 10" loose-fit waist. 12" length. Of horizontally-ribbed white pique, the flat-front dress fits snugly at the bodice and flares at the hips. The front closes with nine pearl buttons and hand-made buttonholes, and the dress features long coat sleeves, and a back box-pleated skirt from below the hips. The dress is richly decorated with rows of hand-made rick-rack that extend down the front, around the side, and up the back, and is repeated at the sleeve edges. Circa 1870. $500/700

83. PETITE WHITE PIQUE DRESS WITH SOUTACHE TRIM

3" shoulder width. 10" length. A semi-fitted jacket dress of horizontally-ribbed white pique with flat front and flared sides features coat sleeves and a snugly fitted back bodice with a box-pleat below the waist. There is a wide collar edged with dainty lace that is repeated on the sleeve edges, and six buttons with loop closures. The entire front, hem, and back collar are embroidered with soutache trim. Circa 1880. $300/500

84. ROYAL BLUE VELVET BONNET

1 1/2" inside head width. Of rich blue velvet that forms into streamers at the sides and is decorated with silk lilies of the valley and blue silk ribbons. Circa 1875. $200/300

85. TEAL BLUE VELVET BONNET

2" inside head width. A vibrant teal blue velvet toque is decorated with black velvet ribbons in corsage style, and surmounted by a tiny black and white feather. Circa 1875. $200/300

86. WOVEN STRAW BONNET WITH AQUA SILK STREAMERS

2" inside head width. The rounded-top woven bonnet is banded with narrow aqua silk ribbons that form into streamers, and decorated with a curly brown feather. With muslin lining. Circa 1870. $200/300

87. WOVEN STRAW BONNET WITH BLACK LACE TRIM

1 3/4" inside head width. A woven bonnet with muslin lining is decorated with a band of zig-zag applied lace with bead highlights, and having black velvet streamers at the back with lace edging. Circa 1870. $200/300

88. Ivory Silk Satin Wedding Gown with Wax Orange Blossoms

5" shoulder width. 9" waist. 20" overall length. The two-piece wedding gown of luxurious ivory silk satin comprises a jacket with dart-shaping and snug fit, narrow sleeves with generous pouf at the shoulder-edge, Alencon lace over-lay at the yoke and collar and lace ruffle at the sleeve edges. The jacket is lined and has inset bone-shaping. Along with flat-front skirt with flared panel shaping, extending into a train at the back, having original attached yellow silk lining, and decorated with a wide panel of Alencon lace below the waist and extending down the sides and bottom, and decorated with a garland of wax orange blossoms and leaves. Circa 1880. $1100/1500

89. Woven Ecru Silk Lady's Fitted Jacket

3" shoulder width. 7" waist. Of fine ecru silk with a delicately woven patterned design, the dart-shaped jacket with rounded neckline has an elongated jacket back with constructed bustle. The neckline is trimmed with a wide embroidered tulle collar that matches the lace that appear on the cuffs and entirely around the jacket bottom edge. Cream silk satin ribbons and bows add further detail. Circa 1870. $300/500

90. Ecru Silk Bonnet with Pale Yellow Buttercup Trim

2" inside width. An ecru silk bonnet with firm buckram lining to give shape, is decorated on the exterior with pleated and arranged silk ribbons and clusters of pale yellow buttercups at the crown and sides. The inside brim is decorated with narrow box-pleated ivory silk ribbon and a very delicate scalloped-edge lace while a little monture of buttercups is placed at the upper left side. Circa 1875. $300/500

91. Fine Ivory Silk Bonnet with Winter-White Silk Ribbons

2". An ivory satin bonnet, with firm inner structure to hold its shape, is luxuriously draped over the sides and back, has a tiny neck ruffle, and is decorated with winter-white satin ribbons

and bows and montures of tiny white flowers. The inside brim is formed of narrow pleats that completely encircle the head, and the bonnet is lined. Circa 1880. $300/600

92. Fine Black Velvet Bonnet with Silk Rose Petals

2 1/2" inside width. A soft black velvet bonnet is actually given a firm inner structure with a buckram form, and features upturned brim with a pleated construction and a heart-shaped crown. The bonnet is decorated with black silk banding and ribbons, black plume, and a spray of delicate silk rosebuds. Circa 1870. $300/500

94. Brown Pressed Flannel Wool Bonnet with Silk Ribbons and Feather

2" inside head width. Of pressed brown flannel wool, the toque-style bonnet has a narrow gold silk edge between the brown wool and the burgundy silk inner ruched lining.

The outside of the bonnet is trimmed with nicely draped silk in the same gold and maroon colors and finished with an elegant white plume. Circa 1880. $300/400

95. Aqua and Bronze Silk Gown with Elongated Jacket
3 1/2" shoulder width. 7" waist. 13" overall length. Made of a felicitous combination of aqua and bronze silk faille, the gown comprises a bodice with silk buttons and having attached jacket with elongated front panels, coat sleeves with wide cuffs and back lappets with pockets. The flat-front skirt with four vertical bands of ruching has an elaborate bustle back and a wide band of double box-pleats at the hem. Contrasting placement of the two silk colors occurs in surprising and pleasing ways to provide decorative elements. Circa 1875. $1200/1500

96. Brown Silk Gown with Elaborate Construction

4" shoulder width. 8" waist. 15" overall length. A bronze-brown silk gown patterned with darker abstract dots that match the color of the trim, features a bodice with dart-shaping, rounded neckline and button-back closures, and fitted sleeves. The flat-front skirt is overlaid with draped fabric to suggest fullness and there is a pleated back skirt with great fullness to allow bustle construction. The two front skirt ruffles form into three ruffles at the back surmounted by a wide bow. Decorative details include brown silk ruching at the neckline and cuffs, little bows at bodice and skirt, bellows pocket with decorative silver buttons to match the costume buttons, and brown silk edging at all ruffles, edges and large bow. Circa 1875. $800/1100

97. Magneta Silk Lady's Gown with Honey-comb Ruching

3 1/2" shoulder width. 7" waist. 12" overall length. A delicate magenta silk gown has a fitted jacket with flared hips, long coat sleeves, and an attached over-skirt that is luxuriously draped at the sides and back to form a demi-train and generous bustle. There is a puffy honey-combedpattern formed by ruching at the upper arms and front skirt panel, a row of narrow pleats at the hem, and fine hand-made lace forming the collar, and edging the jacket, cuffs, over-skirt, and train, with additional dust ruffle on underskirt of train. Circa 1875. $600/900

98. Peach Silk Faille Bonnet with Silk Flower Garland

2" inside head width. An unusual woven straw brim serves as a form for the lavishly draped and folded peach silk faille crown which, in turn, is trimmed with bronze-brown silk ribbons and bow, and beautiful garland of tiny silk flowers and leaves. The bonnet is fully-lined. Circa 1870. $300/400

99. Pressed Wool Felt Flannel Toque

2" inside head width. Of pressed wool felt flannel in taupe color, the classic hat has maroon silk banding, brim-edging, and side bow, Circa 1875. $200/300

100. An Elaborate Peach Silk Lady's Gown with Train
4" shoulder width. 7" waist. 14" overall length. A peach silk two-piece gown features a dart-shaped jacket with square-cut neckline, and coat sleeves. The flat-front under-skirt is edged at the hem with a draped flounce of silk above narrow pleats, and is softened with a gracefully draped over-skirt. The back underskirt extends into a splendid train that is enhanced by the voluminous bustled over-skirt with pleated sides. Fine fringed-edge ruching and lace edge the skirt, train, sleeves, and neckline, with added peach silk bows and streamers. Circa 1875.
$1200/1500

101. Moss-Green Silk Faille Fashion Gown with Decorative Pleats

4" shoulder width. 8" waist. 15" overall. Of very fine silk faille in a delicate shale of green, the two-piece fashion gown features a dart-shaped jacket with snug fit over the hips, lapel collar centering an insert panel with white pearl buttons and hand-made button holes and horizontal metallic braid trim that is repeated around the jacket edges, lapels and cuffs, as well as on the skirt. The flat-front skirt has an insert V-shaped front panel with four rows of narrow-pleats, flanked by horizontal draping around the sides. There are two rows of narrow skirt pleats below the draping that meet with a double-sided band of pleats that extend down each side of the back and continue into an extended train. The skirt has an unusual low bustle at the back with hidden string-adjustable shape. Other details include muslin and lace all-around dust ruffle, tulle collar and silk bows. Circa 1875. $600/900

102. Peach and Bronze-Green Gown with Silk Fringe

3" shoulder width. 6" waist. 12" overall length. Of crisp silk faille, the gown features a fitted peach bodice with attached short jacket that ties at the front above the waist, long sleeves with widened and elaborately constructed cuffs, dart-shaped back that extends to the floor forming into a variant train. The flat-front skirt has a pleated over-panel that encircles even the back of the skirt, capturing the bustle, and the skirt has a demi-train. Decorations include delicate silk fringe at the jacket edge, with three rows at the skirt edge. Circa 1875. $400/600

103. Dainty White Lawn Gown with Rose Silk Trim

3" shoulder width. 7" waist. 11" skirt length. 9" jacket front. Of delicately woven fine white lawn, the two-piece ensemble features a dart-shaped bodice, fitted waist, and flared sides that fit snugly over the hips, and the back is gathered at the waist and falls to a 12" length allowing a bustle-like arrangement. The very long pagoda sleeves and the entire front, neckline and bottom edge of the jacket are finished in multiple rows of fine lace and rose silk ribbon, and a pleated flounce is at the back. The flat-front skirt has a gathered back and a 2" decorative band of alternating lace and rose silk ribbons just above the hem. A matching petticoat is included. Circa 1875. $700/900

105. Brown Kidskin Poupée Boots and Tan Gloves

2 1/2" l. boots. Of soft black kidskin, the boots have side flaps with silver button closures, and tiny heels. Along with tan gloves with separately stitched thumb, scalloped edging. Circa 1870. $300/400

104. Blue Cotton Sateen Gown with Polka Dots

3" shoulder width. 6" waist. 12" overall length. Azure-blue polished cotton two-piece gown with unusual printed pattern of blue and red dots, features a square-cut neckline with collar, dart-shaped jacket that snugly fits the hips, coat sleeves with flared cuffs, and an elaborately constructed skirt with pleated rows of fabric ruffles centered by a large fabric bow at the front and a bustle-back with demi-train. There is red banding at many edges, along with dainty cotton lace edging, and a separate red ruffle at the train. Circa 1870. $700/900

109 back.

109 front.

106. Pressed Wool Felt Flannel Toque with Aqua Blue Silk Ribbons

1 3/4" inside head width. A pressed wool felt flannel toque in winter-white has aqua-blue silk edging, banding, bow and streamers, with tiny rose petals at the inside crown and at the exterior nape. Lined. Circa 1860. $500/700

107. Ivory Bonnet with Aqua Velvet Trim

2" inside head width. The rounded-shape bonnet is constructed of a very fine ribbed material, likely a silk/wool combination with wire-framed brim. There is a draped and folded aqua velvet inner brim, and the same velvet forming a band with draped bow at the exterior. A dainty feather and rose petals add decorative touches. The bonnet has original tulle lining. Circa 1865. $300/500

108. French Aqua Kidskin Boots with Brass Buttons

3". The narrow kidskin boots in unusual aqua color have lappel closures with button-holes and five brass buttons, soft kid soles with darker rims, cream kidskin upper-edge lining. Circa 1870. $200/300

109. Purple Wool Two-Piece Lady's Gown

4" shoulder width. 7" waist. 15" overall length. A two-piece purple wool jacket with dart-shaped snug fit at the waist and over the hips has two pockets, coat sleeves with heavy lace cuffs, six buttons and hand-made button holes. The flat-front skirt has horizontal pleats at the center front flanked by pleated vertical bands that are repeated all around the bottom of the skirt, meet with elaborately constructed bustle at the back and form a train, with muslin and lace dust ruffle. Circa 1870. $400/500

110.1. Brown Wool Felt Flannel Pressed Bonnet

2" inside width. The rich brown wool felt flannel bonnet is given its shape by a pressing method, and has rounded crown and upturned front brim. The hat is decorated with brown silk ribbons that fold artfully around the band forming a rouleaux at the crown and a bow at the nape. The brim is edged with the same brown silk. Circa 1860. $300/500

110. Brown Silk Gown with Shadow Striped Pattern

3" shoulder width. 6" waist. 12" overall length. The three-piece gown of brown silk with lighter-brown shadow-striping has a short fitted jacket with coat sleeves, flat-front skirt, and overskirt with apron front and three-tiered lappets at the back. The gown is edged with black lace at cuffs, apron, and lappets, and has a white lace collar. Circa 1865. $300/500

111. Striped Silk Lady's Gown with Bustle Back

3" shoulder width. 6" waist. 13" overall length. A grey silk fitted gown with very narrow black woven stripes has a very elongated jacket that nearly reaches the hem, with button front, long sleeves, bellows pockets, lace ruffles at the neckline and ruffled cuffs, and bustle back with large black bow. The extended length of the jacket creates a tiered ruffle effect with the under-skirt ruffles which form into demi-train. Circa 1870. $400/600

112. Black Velvet Jacket and Fancy Velvet Bonnet

8" shoulder width. 4 1/2" inside head width of bonnet. The black velvet jacket with coat sleeves, rounded neck, two button closure and beaded decorations, has a quilted silk lining. Along with an extravagant confection of bonnet whose brown velvet form is virtually hidden beneath artfully arranged black velvet bows, black lace over gold fabric, applique silver jewelry, and an intriguing face frame of latticework black crepe. The bonnet is fully lined and has long black velvet streamers. Circa 1875. $500/800

113. Fine Woven Straw Bonnet with Very Elaborate Decorations

4" inside head width. The flat-topped bonnet with wide brim is decorated with a wide brown velvet ribbon edged with black Alencon lace that also forms a bavolet, and with an unusual metallic fabric cluster to simulate leaves. The inside brim is of maroon velvet with a thickly ruffled flounce of pont d'esprit lace. There are black velvet streamers. Circa 1875. $300/500

114. Black Velvet Bonnet with Black Ribbons and Feathers

5" inside head width. A nicely-shaped black velvet bonnet designed to fit neatly to the back of the head, is decorated with a velvet brim trimmed with folded and draped black silk ribbons and feathered plumes, and has long black streamers. Circa 1875. $200/400

116. Three Traditional Coiffes for Poupées
Each sized for wear by 15"-17" poupée. Including black lace coiffe with flat top decorated by finial; rare Normandy coiffe with fine lace trim, and lace cap to be worn under various outer caps. Circa 1875. $400/600

115. Black Silk Lady Gown with Train
3" shoulder width. 6" waist. 11" overall length. A black silk two-piece gown features a fitted jacket with long sleeves and cotton lace collar, above a matching skirt with flat front, pleated border at the hem that extends and forms a long train at the back with attached dust ruffle, and having an overskirt that lends an elegant draped effect. Circa 1870. $400/600

117. Quilted Ivory Silk Bonnet in Wooden Hat Box
2" inside head width. A fine ivory silk is richly padded and quilted, with 2" bavolet falling from the back cap and edged with silk fringe. The wire-framed brim has gathered detail, and is trimmed behind with a double row of looped ribbons. The bonnet is preserved in a wooden hat box that once saw life as a candy container according to its original paper label "Boissier, Boulevard des Capucines, Paris". Circa 1875. $400/500

118. Fine Silk-Thread Woven Fichu and Kidskin Gloves

20"l. fichu. 4" gloves. The fichu, of loosely woven black silk threads has a long silk fringe and an interwoven abstract floral pattern in rich colors. Along with brown kidskin gloves with separately-stitched thumbs. Circa 1890. $200/300

119. Night Shifts and Sacques for Early Dolls

Each is hand-stitched of fine cottons with a variety of needlework techniques, sized for 15"-20" lady dolls. There are three full-length long-sleeved night shifts, and a delicate white day jacket. Circa 1865. (Not photographed). $200/300

120. Collection of Undergarments

Including a 13" length bustle-back collapsible hoop with adjustable drawstrings, three chemises, a night jacket, two pantalets, and two petticoats. Mid-19th century. (Not photographed). $200/300

121. Black Silk Satin Gown with Exceptional Embroidery

3 1/2" shoulder width. 7" waist. 14" overall length. Of luxurious black silk satin, the one piece dart-shaped gown has long coat sleeves with constructed cuffs, V-shaped neckline, and lacing that extends up the entire length. There are long wings that are embroidered with vibrant wildflowers; the embroidery extends entirely around the skirt bottom and on the cuffs. The theatrical style costume is most unique; it is arguable whether the lacing is designed to be in the front or the back. Circa 1880. $500/700

122. Royal Purple Velvet Bodice and Bonnet

4 1/2" shoulders. 7 1/2" waist. Of softest velvet in a rich royal purple color, featuring a bodice with dart-shape, rounded collar, scalloped-shaped lower edge that becomes an extended back tail, 3/4 sleeves, aqua silk bows. Along with matching velvet bonnet with wire frame and a bountiful bouquet of variegated silk flowers on the crown. Circa 1875. $300/400

123. Royal Purple Bonnet Trimmed with Tiny Berries with French Milliner's label

4" width. Designed to sit on the back of the head and frame inside head the face, the wire-framed bonnet is formed of a rich berry-purple with folded pleats, and has a decorative and intricately folded burgundy silk arrangement at the crow that is decorated with a "diamond" buckle and a cluster of tiny red berries. The burgundy ribbons extends entirely around the edge and form into streamers, and a coral braid and black looped design edge the inner brim. With original (illegible) gold French milliner's label. Circa 1875. $500/800

126 back.

126.

124. Aqua Cotton Sateen Dress with Velvet and Belgian Lace Trim
5 1/2" shoulder width. 17" overall length. 16" hips. Of aqua cotton sateen with full lining, the dress has extended princess-style torso with four graduated-length pleats below the hips. A diagonal trim of burgundy velvet and ruffled Belgian lace decorates the torso. The velvet also edges the cuffs and is decorated with a delicate lace that is repeated on the skirt tiers. There is some fading of the aqua fabric. Circa 1880. $600/900

126. Lavender Silk Lady's Dress and Bonnet
4 1/2" shoulder width. 14" overall length. 2 1/2" inside head width. Of luxuriously soft lavender silk satin duchesse, in a rich lavender color, the gown has a flat-front with dart-shaped back, shirring detail at the collar, cuffs, front bodice and extending to the hem which has a band of shirring above three ruffles of silk fringe. At the back is a wide bow of lavender silk. Included is a matching bonnet with wire-framed ruffled brim and floral decoration. Circa 1880. $700/1000

49

127. Ivory Silk Faille Dress with Exceptional Embroidery
7" shoulder width. 21" overall length. Ivory silk faille dress with square cut low neckline edged with self-cording and lace ruffle has a dropped-waist with pleats below the hips, five front self-covered buttons with handmade button holes, sleevelets with lace sous-sleeves, side-back hip pockets. The dress has exceptional raised-embroidery in ivory silk threads depicting a garland vine of flowers and leaves which trails down the front bodice, around the hips sash, sleevelets and pockets and even on the buttons themselves. The gown is decorated with bronze-gold wide ribbon bows at front, back and shoulders. Originally a child's dress but suitable for costuming a plump-bodied bébé about 33"-37". Circa 1880. $300/500

128.

128. Ivory Silk Faille Bavolet Bonnet with Extravagant Lace Ruffle
5" inside head width. Of soft ivory silk faille, the bonnet is formed by a fine wire frame and a richly detailed medallion at the back of the head. Pleated lace and silk ribbon loops frame the face and are framed, themselves, by an extravagant 4" ruffle of silk faille and lace. A 6" silk-edged bavolet protects the back neck, and the silk-lined bonnet is tied with ivory silk ribbons. Circa 1885. $300/400

129. Fine Tulle Bonnet with Flow-Flow Ivory Silk Ribbons
6" inside head width. Of most delicate tulle, the bonnet achieves its shape from

129.

encircling box-pleated ruffles, and is decorated with a cluster of flow-flow silk ribbons and a double row of pleated wide tulle at the crown. The silk ribbons in a braided design form three vertical rows on the back of the head, and then form into streamers. Circa 1875. $300/400

130. Boy's Suit with Leather Suspenders and Brimmed Cap

3 1/2" shoulder width. 6" waist. 8" knee-length pants. The ensemble comprises a nubby linen-like brown jacket with green embroidered edging and button trim, double rows of round buttons at the jacket front and decorating the cuffs; white shirt with detachable collar; black velvet knickers with leather suspenders; and a matching cap to jacket with stiffened black brim. Circa 1885. $700/900

131. Fine Early Pongee Silk Child's Dress with Lace Fanchon Bonnet

7" shoulder width. 19" overall length. A child's dress of pongee silk in a cafe-au-lait color features slightly dropped waist below a box-pleated bodice, rounded wide detachable collar with Alencon lace edging that is repeated at the sleeve edges, tightly gathered skirt forming into a bouffant at hip-length above a row of narrow pleats. There are bone buttons and handmade button holes at he back, and a detachable belt. Also included is a Fanchon bonnet constructed entirely of richly draped and folded delicate lace with a crown of brown silk faille ribbons that form into streamers at the sides. The costume would be suitable for a child doll about 33"-37". Circa 1870. $600/900

132, 133.

134. IVORY SILK SATIN BONNET WITH DELICATE FLORAL PATTERN
3" inside head width. Of softest ivory silk satin known as "satin duchesse", and having a delicately woven design of lavender and rose flowers, the wire-framed ruffled bonnet is decorated with little silk flowers and a silk bow and streamers. Circa 1890. $200/300

132. WHITE PIQUE BÉBÉ DRESS WITH DROPPED WAIST
5" shoulder width. 15" overall length. Of a finely woven pique with waffle-weave pattern and fleecy underside, the princess style dress has a dropped waist, graduated width lapels, pearl button front, coat sleeves, six decorative lappets and a pleated skirt. The lapels, cuffs, lappets and neckline are edged with self-piping, braids, and scalloped edge cutwork, as are the two small pockets at the side hips. Circa 1880. $500/700

133. WHITE PIQUE PRINCESS-STYLE DRESS WITH IVORY SILK BOWS
3" shoulders. 9" overall length. A horizontally-ribbed white pique princess-style dress has flat-front with hook and eye closure, double row of tiny white buttons, coat sleeves with turned-up cuffs of broderie anglaise that match the trim around the hem. The back achieves its shape from a shirred arrangement. The wide rounded collar has soutache embroidery and is edged in a delicate lace, and there are ivory silk faille arranged ribbons at the back and center-front hemline with accent button trim. Circa 1880. $400/600

135. Burgundy and Cream Velvet Bonnet with Beaded Edging

4 1/2" inside head width. A rich confection of burgundy velvet is draped around the sides of the bonnet and forms a brim that is generously padded, has velvet interior brim and is edged in ruby glass prism beads. The back is formed of a lattice-work design of burgundy chenille over a lush cream velvet base, and there is a confection of cream and burgundy velvet and ivory taffeta ribbon at the crown. The original milliner's label "Winters, 489 Fulton St. Brooklyn" is centered in the lining. Circa 1880. $400/500

136. White Cotton Percale Dress with Broderie Anglaise Trim

4" shoulders. 10" overall length. A white cotton percale dropped-waist dress has a rounded collar and sleevelets of broderie anglaise with hand-edged scalloping, and there are two ruffled tiers of broderie anglaise below the hip sash. The sash loops are of a fine embroidered dimity, and the sash and shoulder bows are of magenta silk. Circa 1880. $300/400

137. White Cotton Dress of Broderie Anglaise with Velvet Bonnet

8" shoulder width. 19" overall length. A white cotton dress with a rounded collar and sleevelets formed of broderie anglaise, has a dropped waist with burgundy silk faille sash, and an inset bodice panel with three vertical rows of broderie anglaise, above a gathered skirt whose lower 6" is form of broderie anglaise with a variant pattern, this one of an 8-petaled flower. There are hidden buttons at the back. Along with a superb burgundy velvet bonnet with burgundy satin ruching on the inner brim, and long burgundy silk faille streamers. Circa 1880. $700/1000

139. Blue Velvet and Silk Aqua Bonnet with Paris Label

5" inside head diameter. A wire-framed bonnet with padded and richly draped midnight-blue velvet brim is framed with a looped sky-blue velvet ribbon that forms a large bow at the crown. The bonnet back is a thickly ruched aqua silk in concentric circles, and a plume surmounts all. The interior lining is labeled "M. Malavery Rue l'Universitie Paris". Circa 1880. $400/600

138. Young Child's Dress of Blue Velvet

9" shoulder width. 20" over all length. Of lustrous thick blue velvet, the rounded-neck fully-lined dress features a drop-waist above pleated skirt, and has short caplet sleeves. The neckline is edged with an exquisite embroidered lace fraise that forms into a wide ruffled collar, and matches the 1 1/2" lace ruffle at the sleeve edge. There is a small fabric tear at the back skirt. Circa 1880. $300/500

140. Blue Velvet Dress and Bonnet for Mignonette

2" shoulder width. 4 1/2" overall length. Of simple construction, perhaps a child's work, the blue velvet dress is formed of three straight panels, the two front panels with lining and trimmed with a fine Alencon lace border, cuffs and collar, with aqua silk ribbons at neck and hips, and having a matching toque bonnet with aqua silk banding and bow. Circa 1885. $300/400

141. Blue Silk Two-Piece Dress in the Spanish Mode
5" shoulders. 8" waist. 10" skirt length. Of crisp ice-blue silk, fully lined of nanking cotton, the two-piece gown features a dart-shaped bodice with hook and eye closure under decorative metal buttons that are painted to match the dress, 3/4 coat sleeves with fullness at the shoulders and having Spanish-style braid and lace trim, that matches the trim at the cuffs and lappets. The diamond-shaped lappets hide the waist of the skirt which has a flat-front panel and cartridge-pleated back. Some fraility to silk on bodice. Circa 1875. $200/300

142. Tan Leather Heeled Shoes with Grosgrain Buckles
4 1/2"l. Soft natural brown tan shoes with pointed toes, tan soles, wooden heels, in slip-on style with high vamp with brown grosgrain ribbon and silver buckle. Marked "13", presumably corresponding to Jumeau shoe size. Circa 1885. $300/500

143. Tan Leather Shoes
4 3/4"l. A rich honey-brown color leather with instep straps, brown linen-like edging, brown button closures, cream kidskin lining, and tan soles with darker brown outer edges. Circa 1875. $200/400

144. French Black Leather Shoes, Size 13, Marked C.C.
4 1/4". Of black kidskin with brown silk edging, bows and ankle straps, and having tan soles marked "13" and C.C. (in circle). Circa 1885. $400/500

145. French Leather Shoes with Silver Buckle
3"l. Soft kidskin shoes with ankle straps, button closures, are decorated with fancy silver buckles, and have tan soles. Circa 1884. $300/400

146. Pair of French Shoes Signed Bru Jne, Size 15
5"l. Black leather shoes with leather bows and gold buckles have ankle straps with black button closures and are marked "Bru Jne Paris 14" on the leather soles. Circa 1890. $600/900

147. Vibrant Silk Gown with Original Apron

4" shoulder width. 8" waist. 13" overall length. A vibrant emerald green silk gown has V-shaped neckline with front closure, coat sleeves with black velvet and lace cuffs, with original silk apron of luxuriant pinstripes in purple and rose, with exceptional tri-color woven lace and velvet velvet trim. Circa 1880. $700/900

148. Mauve Velvet and Alencon Lace Coiffe

5" inside head width. Richly draped mauve velvet frames the face of a very lavish lace coiffe, its head back an extravagant confection of folded and draped lace that is both stitched-down and loosely falling, and is decorated with lavender silk ribbons. The cap achieves structure with a stitched buckram lining. Circa 1880. $300/500

149. Fine Leather Boots signed J.R.

2 1/2"l. Black kidskin boots with two sets of ankle straps have brown silk edging and are richly decorated with silver rosettes and black lead closures, and brown silk bows with silver buckles. The tan soles are marked J.B. and "3". Circa 1882. $400/600

150. Fine Cotton Twill Bonnet with Embroidered Floral Medallion

4" inside head width. A tightly woven cotton twill forms a bonnet whose cap-back is embroidered in a rich design of flowers and vines. An arrangement of 3 rows of tulle alternates with three rows of looped ribbons all around the face, and is surmounted by a very high wire-framed shirred crown that is decorated in front and behind with lavish ivory satin ribbons and bows. The bonnet is fully lined and has ivory streamers. Circa 1875. $300/500

151. Ivory Satin Surah Bonnet with An Elaborate Flounce of Lace Ruffles

4" inside head width. With elaborately draped back edged by 2' band of shirring all around the face with S-loop shaped passamenterie trim, the bonnet has a diamond-point border that frames three rows of very lush and thickly-gathered lace. At the crown is an elaborate confection of arranged lace and ivory satin ribbons and bows. The bonnet is fully lined with stiffened muslin for form. Circa 1870. $400/600

152. Plum-Purple Velvet Dress and Bonnet

6" shoulder width. 16" overall length. Of luxurious plum-purple velvet, the button front coat-dress has patterned silk lining, pouf sleeves with constructed gather at the cuff edge to lend an elegant draped effect, relaxed fit, and is decorated with wide bands of appliqued torchon lace. With matching bonnet also trimmed with applique lace and a cluster of organza flowers. Circa 1890. $500/800

153, 154.

153. Ecru Crocheted Dress with Pouf Sleeve Under-Dress

6" shoulder width. 19" length. A cream polished-cotton dress with pouf sleeves achieved by tight cartridge-pleating at the shoulders and gathering at the elbows, is enhanced by a hand-crocheted over-dress with pearl buttons at the back, peach silk satin bows at the shoulders, and velvet peach sash which is captured in a dainty cotton thread zig-zag stitch. A scalloped border edges the hemline. Circa 1890. $200/400

154. White Crocheted Child's Dress with Peach Silk Ribbons

10" shoulder width. 23" overall length. Originally a child's dress but appropriate on dolls 35"-40". Of white open-weave lace crochet designed to be worn with under-dress, the intricately-designed dress has rounded neckline, short sleeves, flared skirt and rose silk draw-ribbons at neckline and high bodice. Circa 1900. $300/400

155. Lace and Rose Silk Bonnet with Regent Street Milliner's Label

4 1/2" inside head width. A narrow wire frame with tulle cap provides the hidden framework for the lavish confection of richly draped embroidered lace that cascades 9" below the nape, and is decorated by two large rose silk satin bows. Circa 1880. $300/500

155.

155. Lace and Rose Silk Bonnet with Regent Street Milliner's Label

4 1/2" inside head width. A narrow wire frame with tulle cap provides the hidden framework for the lavish confection of richly draped embroidered lace that cascades 9" below the nape, and is decorated by two large rose silk satin bows. Circa 1880. $300/500

156. White Pique Jacket-Style Bébé Dress with Cut-work Borders

4 1/2" shoulder width. 14" overall length. Of white-pique in a honeycomb texture, the jacket-style dress has nicely shaped princess-style shape achieved by dart-shaping and flared sides, The faux-jacket has long coat sleeves and encloses the set-in buttoned yoke that has an unusual box-pleated bodice that falls to hip level where it is banded by a wide self sash above box-pleated skirt. The jacket reaches just above the hem at the back and flares with constructed box pleats. The jacket edges, cuffs, skirt hemline and

156, 157, 158.

edge of wide rounded collar are all trimmed with a dainty white cotton scalloped-edge cut-work border. Circa 1880. $500/700

157. WHITE PIQUE DRESS WITH CAPELET COLLAR AND SOUTACHE EMBROIDERY
3 1/2" shoulder width. 12" overall length. The princess-styled dress with full-length dart-shaping at the front, flared sides and box-pleated back captured by a wide back sash, features coat sleeves with wide flared cuffs, and a very large capelet collar. There is very intricate and fine soutache embroidery down the front, around the hem of the dress, at the back sash, on the cuffs, and on the collar. Circa 1870. $700/900

158. WHITE QUILTED PIQUE DAY DRESS FOR LADY DOLL
3 1/2" shoulder width. 11" overall length. Of white pique with fleecy backing and having quilted-like diamond-shape design on the fabric, the flat-front dress has flared skirt sides, is faux-double-breasted, with seven handmade button holes for one actual row of buttons, long coat sleeves, dart-shaped down the entire back with three 1 1/2" box-pleats at the hemline. Pearl buttons and handmade cotton loop-lace provide simple but effective decoration. Circa 1870. $500/700

159. SCALLOPED-EDGE BONNET OF BRODERIE ANGLAISE WITH MAUVE RIBBONS
3" inside head width. The bonnet medallion-back is richly encrusted with embroidered cutwork known as broderie anglaise, and there are two scalloped-edge brims of the same broderie anglaise, separated by yet another band of broderie anglaise that gives dimension to the brims. Four mauve silk taffeta bows decorate the foremost brim. The bonnet is lined. Circa 1875. $300/500

161. Aqua and Cream Pin-Striped Cotton Princess Dress

4" shoulder width. 13" length. Of fine crisp cotton in a pin-stripe design of aqua and cream, the dress features a rolled collar that extends into a button-front flap that extends the entire length of the dress. With 3/4 sleeves, pockets, and a dainty back sash above six long pleats, the dress is decorated with handmade braid and has bone buttons and handmade button holes. Circa 1880. $300/400

160. Blue Cotton Chambray Dress with Wide Collar and Pockets

6" shoulders. 17" overall length. Of a tiny-patterned checkered design in blue and cream, the chambray cotton dress has nine-button front with hand-made button holes, wide rolled collar with pointed tips, long coat sleeves, flat-front with slightly flared sides, dart-shaped back, three double-box kick-pleats at the back. There are two pockets which are outlined in cream braid along with the collar, cuffs, front and kick pleats. The dress appears to have been constructed as a "seamstress sample" as the detail of original trim varies from right and left side, and the three kick pleats each have a variation of trim ranging from double width to single width to none; possibly the dress was offered in degrees of price depending upon trim. Circa 1880. $300/500

162. Tan Leather Shoes with Aqua Silk Rosettes

3 1/2"l. Soft tan kidskin shoes with ankle straps, silver buttons and decorative aqua silk rosettes centering a tiny brown kidskin bow with silver buckle. Circa 1880. $300/400

163. Rose Pin-Stripe Cotton Bébé Dress

3" shoulder width. 8" overall length. The princess-style dress is made of a very narrow pinstripe in rose and cream, with long coat sleeves, hook and eye front closure with five decorative buttons, rounded collar with handmade rick-rack, and dart-shaped back above a row of box pleats at the back hem. Circa 1882 $200/300

164. Red Serge Princess-Style Dress with Box Pleats

4" shoulder width. 11" overall length. Of cherry-red wool serge, the jacket-style princess dress has coat sleeves with flared cuffs decorated with a double triangular appliqué, which repeats as lappets that encircle the back of the dress. The back is dart-shaped and on the side hips are pockets with further lappet trim. A row of box-pleats is all-around the lower skirt, and the dress has pearl buttons and handmade button holes at the center front. The neckline and sleeve tips are edged with lace. Circa 1880. $400/500

165. Rose Cotton Princess Style Dress with Braid Trim

4" shoulder width. 10" overall length. Of pale rose cotton, the princess-style dress has coat sleeves, wide collar with square-shaped back, a row of box-pleats that extends entirely around the lower skirt, dart-shaped back torso, and attached wide all-around hip sash. The dress has hook and eye closures under tiny decorative red buttons. There is a lace ruffle at the neckline and cuffs, and borders of scalloped-edge braid in colorful red, white and blue edge the collar, sleeves, sash, and hem. There is a stain in mid-front torso. Circa 1882. $400/500

166. French Cream Kidskin Boots, Size 7

2 3/4". Soft cream kidskin boots with three pairs of lacing holes, original laces, pom-pom trim have tan soles marked with full-figure of a doll and "7" corresponding to Jumeau bébé size 7. Circa 1885. $300/500

167. French Black Leather Boots, Size 7

2 3/4"l. Of soft black kidskin with glazed finish, the boots have three pairs of lacing holes, original laces, brown pom-poms, and original tan soles impressed with full figure of doll and "7". Circa 1886. $300/500

168. French Brown Leather Boots Marked L.I., Size 9

3" l. Of soft black kidskin, the high boots have 3 pairs of lacing holes, original laces, silk medallion trim, and are marked L.I. (in oval) and "9". Circa 1885. $300/400

169. French Tan Leather Boots Marked L.I., Size 12

4"l. Of tan leather, with scalloped-edge high tops, the boots have five pairs of lacing holes with original laces and are decorated with a silver buckle. Signed L.I. (in oval) and "12". Circa 1885. $300/400

170. Teal Blue Serge Mariner Dress with Dropped Waist
4" shoulder width. 10" overall length. Of a lovely teal or robin's egg blue serge, the dropped-waist dress features wide lapels centering a V-shaped insert panel. There are 3/4 length sleeves and a pleated skirt with hip sash. The lapels, insert panel, cuffs, sash, and skirt edge are decorated with bands of appliqued grosgrain ribbon. The dress has some moth holes. Circa 1880. $400/600

171. Navy Blue Wool Serge Mariner-Style Ensemble
3" shoulder width. 8" overall length. Of navy blue serge the ensemble features a middy-style jacket with single breast-pocket, and a gathered skirt, each decorated with bands of cream grosgrain. There are some motholes. Circa 1880. $300/400

172. Blue Velvet Charlotte Bonnet with Silk Flowers
4" inside head width. Very lush royal blue velvet bonnet is padded and lined with ivory silk satin. The velvet and ivory form a very dominant ruffle around the face and form into a bavolet at the nape. The bonnet is decorated at the crown with a garland of silk flowers and lace, and has a bow and streamers of double-sided blue velvet and silk. Circa 1880. $300/500

173. Aqua Wool Dress with Paisley Panels

3" shoulder width. 9" overall length. Of aqua wool in a diagonal twill weave, the bébé dress has inserted panels of paisley-like woolen weave, the back panel with double box-pleats at the center torso with aqua wool inside panels. The dress has paisley and aqua alternating sleeve panels, nine brass buttons with handmade button holes, and superb detail of draped Alencon lace in two rows down the front panel, encircling the hem, and around the neckline and cuffs. Circa 1880. $300/400

174. Aqua Silk Faille and Knit Bébé Dress and Bonnet

4" shoulder width. 12" overall length. The dropped-waist dress is an unusual combination of finely knit bodice and patterned-silk faille box-pleated skirt with wide draped sash that forms a large bow at the back. The bodice, designed to fit snugly, has long sleeves with wide wrists. There is feather-stitching on the bodice and frivolous tassels on the sleeves. Insluded is a brown pressed-velvet bonnet with duckbill brim, decorated with a silver buckle and aqua silk ribbons. Circa 1885. $700/900

175. Sea-Blue Woolen Dress with Feather-Stitching

5" shoulder width. 13" overall length. To fit Bébé Jumeau, size 10 and likely from the workshops of Ernestine Jumeau. Of fine lightweight wool, the slightly-dropped-waist dress has a box-pleated bodice that is trimmed with cream feather-stitch embroidery which repeats on the cuffs of the long sleeves. The skirt is gathered all-around, more densely at the back, and the hem is trimmed with a wide band of broderie anglaise with scalloped cut-work at the very bottom edge. Circa 1888. $600/800

176. Pin-Striped Velvet Dress with Argentan Lace Collar and Knit Cap

5" shoulder width. 16" overall length. A fine silk-velvet fabric in a very narrow pinstripe design of black and ivory has slightly dropped waist below a pleated bodice, rounded collar with self-edging, elbow-length gathered sleeves with lace-edged sleeve bands, and a flat-front skirt slightly flared at the sides with one box-pleat at the back. The dress is trimmed with Argentan lace at the yoke and bands of scalloped cotton cutwork at the cuffs and hem. Included is a knit bonnet with scalloped-edge brim and shaded ivory silk ribbons. Circa 1885. $400/500

177. Cream Velvet Bonnet with Monture of Long-Stemmed Wildflowers

4" inside width. Richly draped and arranged lustrous cream velvet forms the cap-back of the ruffled-brim bonnet that is decorated with bronze-green silk streamers and ribbons, and generous monture of long-stemmed white wild-flowers that appear to cascade over the front brim in a charming manner. Circa 1890. $400/500

178. TEXTURED IVORY SILK BONNET WITH RUCHING AND RUFFLES

3 1/2" inside head width. Of textured ivory silk, the capote-style bonnet has a luxurious arrangement of three rows of lace ruffles that extend the entire inside circumference of the head, and having a bouquet of silk ribbons at the crown. Circa 1880s. $300/400

179. BLACK LEATHER SHOES FOR BÉBÉ JUMEAU, SIZE 11

3 1/2"l. Of black leather with brown over-cast edging, ankle straps with button closures, brown silk ribbon trim, and marked "12 Paris Depose" with bee symbol. Jumeau, circa 1890. $300/500

180. BROWN METALLIC FINISH SHOES, SIZE 13

4 1/4"l. Of a rich metallic brown with overcast edging, the shoes have ankle straps with silver button closures, and are decorated with brown silk bows. Signed with full figure of a doll and "13". Circa 1885. $300/400

181. BLACK LEATHER SHOES FOR BÉBÉ JUMEAU, SIZE 14

4 1/2"l. Of black leather with ankle straps, black button closure, brown silk ribbons, and tan soles marked "Park Depose 14" and with bee symbol. Jumeau, circa 1890. $300/500

182. AQUA SILK AND CREAM CASHMERE PRINCESS-STYLE DRESS

3 1/2" shoulder width. 9" overall length. The princess-style dropped-waist dress features sides, back and sleeves of creamy cashmere, and a center panel and skirt of aqua silk faille that is richly draped and folded at the bodice and formed into narrow box pleats at the skirt. There are extended "tails" of cashmere at the back that are gathered into a flounce and trimmed with an aqua silk bow. The aqua bows are repeated at the wrists, and there is a lace ruffle at the wrists and throat. A lace and pleated muslin dust ruffle is hidden beneath the hem. There are a few moth holes. Circa 1882. $700/900

183. CREAMY VELVET DRESS WITH VELVET PLUSH POM-POM BERET

4 1/2" shoulder width. 14" overall length. 4" inside head width. Of lustrous soft shadow-striped velvet and silk combination fabric, the dress has a fitted yoke, gathered bodice with ruffled upper edge, slightly dropped relaxed waist, cartridge-pleated skirt all around, and long sleeves that are very full and gathered at the shoulders, and tapering to a narrow width at the cuffs. Included with the dress is a silk plush beret with gold braid edging, decorated with tri-color silk pom-poms and a white feather. Circa 1880. $400/600

184. Burgundy Silk Faille and Knit Bébé Dress and Bonnet

2 1/2" shoulder width. 7" overall length. A dropped-waist dress with bodice of maroon knit decorated with embroidered dots, and trimmed with tassels and lace-edged cuffs and neckline, has a box-pleated burgundy silk skirt with embossed patterns and pleated muslin under-skirt. A wide maroon silk hip sash ties at the back in a wide bow. Included is the original lace-covered maroon-silk covered bonnet with burgundy silk bows at the crown and a flounce of lace and looped red ribbons around the forehead. Circa 1885. $700/900

185. Boy's Two-Piece Velvet Suit with Braid and Tassel Trim

3 1/2" shoulder width. 8" waist. 4" length jacket. 5"length short pants. Comprising a burgundy velvet jacket trimmed with colorful braid and tassels, along with black velvet knee-length pants with colorful braid along the sides. Circa 1880. $400/500

186. Tiny Woolen Zouave Costume for Mignonette

To fit 5" mignonette. Features a navy blue woolen jacket with red soutache embroidery, red knee-length pants, cream leggings, and having an original blonde mohair wig and red wool cap. Some moth holes. Circa 1880. $300/400

187. Ivory Cashmere Wool Dress with Straw Bonnet

3 1/2" shoulder width. 9" overall. A fine soft cashmere wool forms a bébé dress with fitted yoke, pleated bodice with dropped waist, gathered skirt, faux suspenders, and pouf sleeves. The suspender edges and yoke are decorated with delicate cream appliqués. Included is a tightly woven straw bonnet with tulle overlay, rose satin banding and fluted ivory silk lining. Circa 1890. $500/700

188. Ivory Silk Princess-Style Dress with Elaborate Construction

4" shoulder width. 9" overall length. Of luxurious ivory silk satin duchess, the dress has a center front panel and wide hip sash of tiny rose petals on a brown background, framed by lace bretelles that extend over the shoulders. The sleeves, sides and back of the dress are of ivory silk, as is the box-pleated lower skirt. The dress back has narrow pleats at the top above a panel of tight ruching and decorated by a flounce of ivory silk. The lace bretelles continue into a wide back collar edge and the lace is repeated at the cuffs and lower skirt pleats. Circa 1884. $700/900

190. Woven Straw Bonnet and Black Leather Shoes with Shop Label

7" outside brim. 3" inside head width. 3" l. shoes. The woven straw bonnet with flat-top and wide brim is edged with cream grosgrain ribbon and has a wide ivory silk band and bow, stamped "7" inside. Along with black leather shoes with brown overcast stitching, brown silk rosettes, silver button closures, leather soles incised with figure of doll and "A La Providence, 74 Rue de Rivoli Paris", and "8". Circa 1885. $300/400

191. Pressed Felt-Flannel Toque with Silk Ribbon Bands

3" inside head width. Of a dark sage green, the pressed felt flannel bonnet has slightly rounded crown and upturned sides of the brim. There is a ribbed-silk banding and brim-edging with side ribbon held by a silver clasp. Circa 1880. $200/300

189. Green Plaid Silk Dress with Green Velvet-Brimmed Bonnet

5" shoulder width. 12" waist. 13" overall length. Green silk taffeta plaid dress with dart-fitted bodice and dropped waist has modified pagoda-style sleeve with box-pleats at the shoulders, and a gathered skirt below a self ruffle. The dress is decorated with narrow velvet bands at the rounded neckline that are repeated at the wrists, and an attached wide green velvet sash with large back bow. There is also an accompanying bonnet with wide green velvet brim and ivory floral-patterned silk faille crown. Circa 1890. $500/800

192. Wide-Brimmed Ivory Velvet Bonnet
8" overall width. 3" inside head width. A wire-framed bonnet with flat-top and graduated width of brim (4" at the crown and 2" at the nape), is richly covered with soft cream velvet, and decoarted with ivory silk band and bows and a white plumed feather. There is a tulle and silk lining. Circa 1890. $300/400

193. Creamy Velvet Dress with Velvet Plush Pom-Pom Beret
4 1/2" shoulder width. 14" overall length. 4" inside head width. Of lustrous soft shadow-striped velvet and silk combination fabric, the dress has a fitted yoke, gathered bodice with ruffled upper edge, slightly dropped relaxed waist, cartridge-pleated skirt all around, and long sleeves that are very full and gathered at the shoulders, and tapering to a narrow width at the cuffs. Included with the dress is a silk plush beret with gold braid edging, decorated with tri-color silk pom-poms and a white feather. Circa 1880. $400/600

194. Brown Velvet Dress with Aqua Silk Pleated Panels
5 1/2" shoulder width. 14" overall length. A rich sienna-brown velvet jacket-style dress has double-pleated lapels that center a panel of very narrow silk satin pleats which are repeated at the center front skirt. The brown velvet forms into jacket tails at the dart-shaped back and is trimmed with aqua silk pleats. The lower skirt back is box-pleated and the coat-sleeves are trimmed with bronze-gold silk ribbons and bows which are repeated at the shoulders and as a sash. There is a shirred ruffle at the neckline. Circa 1885. $600/900

195. Golden Silk Dress with Woven Blue-Edged Leaves

5 1/2" shoulder width. 15" overall length. Of an intense-golden silk with interwoven design of blue-edged leaves, the dress features a box-pleated bodice front and flat-panel bodice back, slightly-dropped waist with a center box-pleat framed by all-around 1" pleats. The dress has very full long sleeves with box-pleats at the shoulders and gathered wrist bands that are trimmed with bands of lace and ivory satin ribbons and bows. The trim is repeated at the rounded neckline with a ruffled band of lace that continues down the sides of the bodice. There is an ivory sash with streamers, and a lace border at the hemline. Circa 1885. $800/1100

196. Aqua Silk and Velvet Bébé Dress with Matching Fleeced Plush Bonnet

5 1/2" shoulder width. 14" overall length. An aqua silk dress with fitted yoke, gathered bodice, set-in yet relaxed waist, gathered skirt, has attached faux-jacket in a very thick lush aqua velvet with silk-lined lapels, modified Juliette sleeves with pouf-gathered upper sleeves and straight lower sleeves. The dress is trimmed with a very fine embroidered tulle with arched and scalloped edge, forming a border at the yoke and an overlay of the skirt. The dart-shaped jacket back has four tails that extend to the skirt length. Included is a matching bonnet with very high crown, having aqua plush velvet on the outside, and pleated aqua silk interior, with aqua silk ribbons and flower trim. Circa 1888. $1500/2000

197. White Lace Dress with Bertha Collar
7" shoulder width. 18" overall length. Originally a child's dress but suitable for costuming a 30"-33" doll. Constructed of alternate bands of embroidered white tulle with beading having pale pale green drawn ribbon, square-cut neckline with lace edging, very wide ruffled Bertha collar, pouf sleeves with bands. Circa 1890. $300/400

198. Splendid Aqua Silk "Bird Nest" Bonnet
9" brim. 4 1/2 " inside head width. Pale aqua silk bonnet with wire frame for shaping is lavishly covered with added casually-woven straw interlocked with fine wire netting. There are six tiers of ruffles on the exterior of the bonnet. The interior brim is decorated with two clusters of silk flowers, each within an arrangement of clustered straw to suggest a bird's nest. On one side is a crocus bouquet, and on the other pink rosebuds. The interior of the hat is silk lined, and there is an ivory satin bow that extends over the brim. Circa 1890. $500/700

199. Petite Blue Silk Bébé Dress with Lace Trim
2" shoulder width. 6" length. Of soft pale blue silk satin, the square-collared dress features a dropped-waist with drawstring at the hips, and is decorated with a lavish band of lace at the bodice that forms into widely flared sleevelets. A

band of lace is repeated at the hem, and the dress is trimmed with blue silk bows and silver metallic appliqué trim. Circa 1890. $300/400

200. Petite Ivory Silk Spanish Costume with Cape
2 1/2" shoulder width. 6" waist. 8" overall. Of creamy silk satin, the ensemble comprises jacket with narrow long sleeves, long trousers, and collared cape, each decorated with gold metallic thread and beading in a very elaborate manner, including heavily encrusted epaulets and medallions. Circa 1900. $300/400

201. Aqua Silk Satin Bébé Dress with Lace Edging
3 1/2" shoulder width. 11" length. Of softly-draped aqua silk satin, the dress has a slightly-dropped waist, long sleeves with wide bands, gathered skirt, pearl button and loop closure at the back, and is decorated with embroidered tulle lace with scalloped edge at the bodice, cuffs and hemline, with a row of feather-stitching, with ivory sash and attached petticoat. Circa 1890. $500/700

203. Very Fine Winter-White Silk Bride's Bonnet with Three-Ruffled Tulle Brim

4" inside head width. A pale-white ivory bonnet is given shape by a hidden wire frame and buckram lining. The bonnet back is lavishly draped and has a lace-laden bavolet. Textured ivory silk ribbons are draped around the sides and form large bows at the crown and nape. There is a cluster of small white silk leaves at the crown, and the face is framed by three most delicate tulle ruffles with lace edging. Circa 1885. $400/500

202. Coral Silk Dress with Detachable Collar

5" shoulder width. 15" overall length. Of lustrous coral silk satin duchesse the dress features a bodice with set-in lace panel, rounded neckline, set-in relaxed waist, very-full sleeves with box-pleats at the shoulders and wide fitted cuffs, draped sash with a very wide bow at the back, and gathered skirt. There is a detachable collar that falls nearly to the waist, having diamond-point edging, and a wide ruffled lace edging that matches the front panel. Circa 1885. $600/800

204. Curly Woven Bonnet in Pale Rose

9" brim. 3" inside head width. A wide-brimmed straw bonnet with curled tips is tinted an unusual pale rose color, with richly draped

rose satin band and bow. The interior brim is lined with rose georgette and there is muslin lining inside the cap. Circa 1890. $300/500

205. Magenta Velvet Dress with Lace Collar
4" shoulders. 12" overall length. A silky velvet dress in vibrant magenta color has a fitted yoke and rounded neckline above a high-waist skirt that achieves its fullness from generous pleats and box-pleats all-around. The very full sleeves are edged with lace as is the neckline, and the cutwork and embroidered tulle collar generously covers the full bodice and is emphasized with a magenta silk bow. Circa 1890. $400/500

206. Vibrant Silk Magenta Dress and Bonnet with Red Silk Trim
6" shoulder width. 15" overall length. A magenta silk satin dress with gathered bodice for fullness, set-in yet relaxed waist, and pleated skirt, has very full sleeves with cartridge pleats at the shoulders. The dress is decorated with scalloped-edge torchon lace at the hemline and cuffs, and has red silk ribbon trim with embossed designs and scalloped edging forming a waist sash with long streamers, and decorating the collar and cuffs. Included is a magenta silk bonnet with beautifully-draped brim, decorated with red silk ribbons and bows and pale magenta feather. Circa 1890. $600/900

207. Brown Dropped-Waist Dress with Maroon Silk Ribbons

4" shoulder width. 12" overall length. A textured fabric of wool and silk combination has maroon velvet edging at rounded neckline and pouf sleeves, pleated front and back bodice, dropped waist with ruching at the hips, and maroon silk bows at the left front and back shoulder. Circa 1885. $200/300

208. Maroon Wool Capelet Coat with Unusual Scallop Design

4 1/2" shoulder length. 11" overall length. Of a fine lightweight maroon wool, the one-piece coat-dress has a flat-front with tiny silver buttons and handmade button holes above a dropped-waist, shirred and gathered skirt, full sleeves with shirring at the cuffs lending a honey-comb like effect. There is a waist-length over-cape with detailed shirring at the collar, and decorative diamond-points at the bottom edge of both the cape and the skirt. A black satin bow ties the cape and there is a black satin sash and bow at the hips. Circa 1885. $300/400

209. Maroon Wool Dropped-Waist Dress with Bertha Collar

4 1/2" shoulder width. 15" hips. 11" overall length. Lightweight maroon wool with fitted yoke beneath a very wide Bertha collar that extends entirely around the back, dropped-waist with blouson styling, pleated skirt, pouf sleeves with bands. The dress is decorated with rows of narrow black velvet on the collar and cuffs, applique cotton lace on the collar, and a black silk sash with large back bow. Circa 1895. $300/500

210. Four Pairs of French Doll Shoes

Comprising 3" pair of black leather with silver buckles and ankle straps; 3" narrow-soled early shoes of black leather; 3 1/4" pair of black leather shoes with pom-poms and ankle straps; and 2" very worn red silk shoes, one with original sole labeled Bébé Jumeau in gold lettering, Size 6 (other sole missing). Circa 1885. $300/500

211. GEORGETTE DRESS WITH VELVET POLKA DOTS

4" shoulder width. 9" overall length. A sheer georgette over coral under-dress is decorated with maroon velvet polka dots, and has a lace collar at the rounded neckline, and a wide maroon silk sash and maroon silk shoulder bows. Circa 1885. $300/400

212. BLACK VELVET AND SILK PRINCESS-STYLE DRESS WITH VELVET BONNET

4" shoulder width. 12" overall length. 3" inside head width. A princess-style dress with black silk front panels centered by a row of six silk-covered buttons and handmade button holes is framed by black velvet sides, back and long sleeves. The dart-shaped back has deeply-formed scallops at the hips with silk banding, above a pleated lower skirt, and there is a lace ruffle at the wrists and neckline. Along with a black velvet bonnet with richly-draped construction decorated with a red silk plaid ribbon. Circa 1884. $400/600

213. PETITE IVORY SILK FAILLE COAT AND BONNET FOR BABY

2" shoulder width. 8" overall length. Of ivory silk faille, the baby's long coat has feather-stitching on the collar, sleeves and hem, and drawn-ribbon detail on the sleeves. The coat is fully-lined as is the lace-edged bonnet with embroidery and drawn-work. Circa 1900. $200/300

215. Three Pairs of Leather Shoes
Comprising 3" black kidskin with kidskin bows and silver buckles, ankle strap, unmarked; 3" pair of black leather with silk bows and lace ties on ankle straps, marked "Cremer 240 Regent St." and 3 1/2" leatherette with brown silk rosettes. Circa 1895. $500/600

216. Ivory Silk Satin Duchess Bonnet
3" inside head width. A wire-framed bonnet is constructed with elaborately draped folds at the bonnet back, captured by a band of same silk. The wire-framed brim has elaborate ruffles and fringe, and is further trimmed with a large ivory satin bow at the crown which extends to form long streamers. Circa 1885. $300/500

214. Purple Silk Dropped Waist Dress
4" shoulder width. 11" overall length. A purple silk dropped-waist dress with gathered yoke above a blouson bodice features two rows of box pleats from below the hips, and Juliette sleeves. The dress is decorated with magenta silk bows at the shoulders, and two rows of scalloped-edge Argentan lace separating the box-pleated skirt panels. Age uncertain, antique materials. $300/500

217. Woven Straw Bonnet with Bronze Silk Ribbons

5" inside head width. Designed to perch atop the head, the woven curly straw is tinted amber-brown, and is decorated with matching shaded-toned wide ribbons in an elaborate flounce, with brown feathered ornaments. Circa 1890. $300/500

218. Black Woven Bonnet with Silk Rose Garland

6" brim. 2" inside head width. An elaborately woven black bonnet is decorated with a garland of dainty pink and ivory roses and rose petals with leaves. An interior label reads "Dache, Paris/New York". In the 1890 manner, age uncertain. $300/400

219. Ivory High-Waisted Dress with Matching Bonnet

3 1/2" shoulder width. 12" overall length. An ivory dress of silk and wool combination with textured detail has a fitted yoke above gathers that reach the full-length of the dress, high rounded collar, pouf sleeves with fitted lining to maintain the fullness, wide embroidered cut-work collar with scalloped edging, feather-stitching at the hem, and a decorative ivory silk ribbon. Included is an ivory woolen cap with cut-work lace back and bavolet, ruching details on the sides, and generous ivory silk bows. Circa 1890. $400/500

220. Pair, Leather Shoes Marked "Eden Bébé Paris", Size 11

3 1/2"l. Soft kidskin black shoes with brown over-cast stitching and brown pom-poms, have ankle straps with tiny silver buttons. The leather soles are impressed "Eden Bébé Paris" and "11". Circa 1890 $200/300

221. French Leather Shoes with High Ankle Straps

3 1/2" black leather with brown overcast stitching, large brown silk rosettes and brown laces, signed with full figure of doll and "9". Circa 1890. $300/400

223. Woven Straw Bonnet with Milliner's Label

3" inside head width. 6" brim width. A tightly-woven narrow bonnet with slightly-concave top has very narrow brim at the nape that widens to a generous crown. The outside of the bonnet is decorated with a rose satin bow, and the inside brim is lace covered with a corsage of rose silk flowers and bows. A partial gilt-lettered French milliner's label remains. Circa 1890. $300/400

222. Red Silk Dress with Bertha Collar and Bonnet

4 1/2" shoulder width. 14" overall length. Red silk dress with pleated yoke encircled by a lace Bertha collar, has pouf sleeves with dart-shaping and wide lace sleeve bands, and a pleated loosely-fitting skirt that falls from beneath the collar. There is a border of lace at the hem, and red silk bows at the yoke. Along with a red silk wire-framed bonnet with lace-edging, petal-shaped cap back, and decorated with red silk ribbons and a burgundy plume. Circa 1900. $400/500

224. Two Pairs of Jumeau Shoes

Comprising 2" brown leather shoes with silk rosettes, signed "E. Jumeau, Med d'Or Paris" amd "5"; and 2" brown leather shoes signed "Paris Depose" with bee symbol. Circa 1885 and 1890. $400/500

225. Red Silk Faille Boy's Suit and Cap

4" shoulder width. About 10" overall. The three-piece ensemble, of rich red silk faille, comprises middy-style jacket with ivory silk collar trimmed with braid and red ribbons, matching knickers with draw-string waist and legs, and a sailor cap with feather-stitch and white pom-pom. Circa 1900. $400/600

226. Two Costumes for Petite Dolls

Each 1 3/4" shoulder width. Comprising 1"l. muslin dress with short sleeves and striped blue ribbon banding on skirt and bodice; and 7"l. batiste baby gown with lace trim. Circa 1915. $200/300

226.1. Coral and Red Cotton Sateen Dress with Wide-Brimmed Bonnet

4" shoulder width. 13" overall length. Cotton sateen dress with ivory pleated yoke, coral blouson bodice, wide collar and pleated skirt, very full red sleeves. There is braid and lace trim on the collar and sleeves and an ivory bow with silver buckle. The red cotton sateen bonnet has scalloped edging and lace brim, and is decorated with ivory bows. $400/500

228. Woven Straw Bonnet with Pink Marguerites
5" overall width. 2 1/2" inside head width. A woven flat-topped bonnet with wide upturned brim is decorated with pink marguerites and a rouleaux of ivory satin, with coral bow at the back. Circa 1900. $200/300

229. Dainty Petite White Mull Dress and Cap
2" shoulder width. 6" overall length. A delicate mull fabric is transfer decorated with abstract pale red pattern, and forms a dainty dress with fitted yoke, wide Bertha collar, pouf sleeves, gathered skirt that falls from the yoke, and a matching wide-brimmed cap. There is lace-edging at the collar, cuffs, and hat brim. Circa 1890. $300/400

227. Dainty Rose Silk Dress with Silk and Velvet Bonnet
6" shoulder width. 14" length. The delicate rose silk dress features a set-in yoke with lace overlay at both front and back, slightly-dropped-waist with blouson bodice with faux-suspenders, ruffled two-tier pink silk skirt, and pouf sleeves with ruffled edges. The dress is trimmed with narrow borders of lace at sleeves, suspenders and skirt ruffles and there is a pale rose bow at the yoke. Along with a rose velvet and sateen bonnet with frail georgette inner brim, and rose streamers. Circa 1890. $600/900

230. Rose Silk Dress for Mignonette
1 1/4" shoulder width. 3" length. A rose silk dress with princess-styling has self-ruffles all-around the front opening, hem, collar, and sleevelets. There is a large bow at the back hips. Circa 1885 $300/400

231. Petite Cotton Kimono with Asian Theme
2 1/2" shoulder width. 7" length. A printed cotton kimono with images of ships, cherry blossoms, and various other symbols in rich colors, has a silk sash and blue cotton edging. Circa 1900. $200/300

232. Rose Silk Middy Dress with Gilt Anchors
5" shoulder width. 12" waist. 14" overall length. Of rose sateen with interwoven horizontal striping, the sleeveless dress features a box-pleated bodice with self-banded neckline, set-in waist, box-pleated front skirt with wide-gored panels at the sides and a gathered skirt at the back. With short matching middy jacket have rose-silk lapels with lace overlay, Juliette sleeves with gathered fullness at the shoulders, lace-covered lower sleeves, and decorations of rose silk ribbons, gilt anchors and rose silk-covered buttons down the sides of the skirt. $700/900

234. Delicate Rose Cotton Bonnet

6" width. 6" height. The delicate rose cotton bonnet is designed to accommodate a coiffure that is arranged high on the head. The cap fits atop the coiffure although it maintains its own structure from a hidden frame inside the cap. It is decorated with sunburst-shaped ruching and has silk bows at each side. Circa 1915. $200/300

233. Delicate Patterned Mull Summer Dress and Bonnet

6" shoulder width. 12" adjustable waist. 20" overall length. The delicate muslin gown is printed with shaded roses and leaves, and features a rose silk collar and black velvet ribbon drawn-work at the bodice, sleeves, waist, and skirt. The sleeves are edged with lace. Along with a curly woven white straw bonnet with rose silk ribbons. Circa 1890. $700/900

235. Cotton Print Dress with Lace Bertha Collar

4" shoulder width. 11" length. A dainty white cotton dress with interwoven pattern is printed with delicate rose flowers, and features a set-in yoke with tucks above a gathered full bodice with dropped waist, and two-tiered ruffled skirt with constructed tucks. The dress has puffed sleeves with lace edging. There is an embroidered tulle Bertha collar that extends around the entire dress. Circa 1890. $300/400

236. Fleecy Lambswool Bonnet with Silk Ribbons

4" inside head. In a rich creamy color, the unusual fleecy bonnet has double self-ruffle with three rows of braid at the back of the head, and a plethora of ribbons and bows. A patterned bow at the center crown is framed by an aqua bow on one side and a mauve bow on the other, and there is a peach silk bow at the inside brim. Circa 1890. $200/300

237. Rose Flannel Coat with Wide Lace-Edged Collar in Presentation Box

4 1/2" shoulder width. 9" overall length. Of soft rose flannel with cream flannel lining, the coat features a fitted yoke above a box-pleat, with three pearl buttons in handmade button holes, and having very full sleeves with wide fitted cuffs, and very large collar with a 2" border of beautiful ruffled lace. The coat is presented in a lovely box with decorative paper covers and lithograph image. Circa 1910. $400/500

238. Delicate Rose Cotton Dress and Black Velvet Bonnet

5" shoulder width. 13" overall length. Of very delicate cotton, the pale rose dress has an inset lace yoke, fitted bodice with decorative buttons, sash, lightly-gathered skirt with ruffled hem. Along with a black velvet cloche with patterned ivory taffeta ribbon and lace edging (inside brim fabric worn). Circa 1915. $200/300

239. Patterned Cotton Two-Piece Dress

5" shoulder width. 9" waist. 15" overall length. Fine muslin two-piece gown with transfer-print features a hip-length fitted jacket with back darts, long sleeves with gathered cuffs, set-in waist band of long skirt with ruffle at hemline, buttons and handmade button holes. There is a decorative band of compatible darker-toned fabric at the placket and bottom edge of the jacket as well as the cuffs and skirt, and a ruffle at the neckline. Circa 1880. $400/500

240. Cream Muslin Two-Piece Dress with Lace Trim

6" shoulder width. 14" overall length. A delicate muslin dress with transfer-design of abstract petals features a rounded neckline with collar, pouf sleeves, and inset bands of handmade lace on both the bodice and the skirt. The skirt is drawn up into a flounce at each side, suggesting the possibility of an underskirt at one time. Circa 1880. $200/300

241. Three Fine Knit Bonnets with Intricate Patterns

Includes wide-brimmed hat with 11" brim and 3 1/2" inside head width in pink and green stripes with popcorn like cap, trimmed with rose silk ribbons; cream knit bonnet with bavolet decorated with rose silk drawstring ribbons and peach bow; and thickly-knit cream bonnet with rose fringed edging. Circa 1890. $300/500

242. Pale Rose Cotton Dress with Broderie Anglaise Collar and Cuffs
4" shoulder width. 13" overall length. Pale rose cotton dress with rounded neckline, coat sleeves, dropped waist, constructed box pleats at front and back torso trimmed with the daintiest of red feather-stitching, narrow skirt pleats, is decorated with a dainty white scalloped-edge collar and cuffs in broderie anglaise, and a red sash matches the feather-stitching. Circa 1885. $300/400

243. Rose and Cream Cotton Striped Dress with Embroidery
Pin-striped rose and cream cotton dress with dropped-waist, box-pleated bodice, gathered skirt, very generous full sleeves, with white bands of ruffled white cotton at the yoke, collar, sleeves and skirt. The white ruffles are edged with overcast rose stitching and have delicately embroidered rose flowers. Circa 1900. $300/400

244. Patterned Rose Cotton Sateen Dress with Matching Bonnet
5" shoulder width. 13" overall length. A lovely fabric with lustrous sheen features abstract shades of rose and cream with dainty blue and pink flowers, having rounded neckline with ruffled collar, sleevelets, dropped-waist, and skirt with two tiers of ruffles. There is a band of ruching above the center front waist and and at the back, and lace edging on collar, sleeves and each skirt ruffle. A wire-framed bonnet is decorated with peach silk streamers and cream silk pom-poms. Circa 1885. $400/500

246. Two Fancily Woven Straw Bonnets
Each about 2" inside head width. Of woven straw, each bonnet has an elaborate confection of ruffles, curls, borders, and flowers, all made of straw. Circa 1900. $300/400

247. Blue Flannel Wool Dress with Featherstitching and Aqua Silk Bonnet
3" shoulder width. 10" length. Of fine flannel wool in a blue/cream muted plaid, the dress features a high waist with constructed tucks embroidered with blue feather-stitching that is repeated on the cuffs of the elbow-length full sleeves. There is an aqua silk satin bow at the shoulder, which matches the aqua silk bonnet with lace edging and silk flower trim. Circa 1890. $400/500

245. Golden Nubby Cotton Dress with Brown Velvet Trim
3 1/2" shoulder width. 9" overall length. Of a fine golden color, the unusual nubby-textured fabric creates an especially pleasing look, having set-in brown velvet V-shaped yoke edged with feather-stitching that is repeated on the velvet cuffs of the wide gathered sleeves. The wide-pleated bodice extends to a dropped waist with relaxed fit and forms into a gathered skirt that is trimmed with a thickly knit brown sash with tassel ends. Circa 1890. $500/700

248. Two Unusual Silk Ruffled Bonnets in Cord-du-Roi
4" inside head width. The identically constructed bonnets are a pleasing combination of fabric and color choices, each having cord-du-roi (corduroy) gathered back, and a double ruffle silk brim. Including one with maroon and red colors, and another is navy blue with aqua. Circa 1890. $300/500

249. Mauve Cotton Dress with Black Feather-Stitch Embroidery

4" shoulder width. 9" waist. 11" overall length. A textured mauve cotton two-piece dress has fitted bodice with three wide box pleats decorated with vertical feather-stitching, wide coat sleeves with wrist buttons, slightly-gathered front and widely gathered back skirt, black velvet stitched-on belt. Circa 1885. $200/300

250. Plaid Cotton Pinafore Dress with Pockets and Fancy Bonnet in the Flora McFlimsey Style

7" shoulder width. 17" overall length. A tightly-woven pinafore dress with fitted yoke, gathered full bodice, long sleeves with constructed cuffs, set-in waist band with back ties, and skirt that is tightly gathered at the center front and has flat-panel sides and lightly gathered skirt back. There are two pockets, and a muslin and embroidered tulle collar. Included with the dress is a wire-framed wide-brimmed bonnet lavishly adorned with miniature silk flowers and leaves. Circa 1890. $500/800

251. Blue and White Gingham Dress with Navy Blue PInaforre
4 1/2" shoulder width. 15" overall length. Sturdy gingham cotton in a tiny blue and white checkered pattern, has rounded neckline, full sleeves with fitted cuffs, lace edging on neckline and cuffs, and a navy blue polka dotted pinafore with applied braid designs that ties at the back. Circa 1900. $400/600

252. Cream Cotton Pinafore with Blue Chambray Borders
6" shoulder width. 14" overall length. The textured cotton pinafore with blouson bodice and gathered skirt is decorated with borders of blue chambray having red embroidered and scalloped edging. The borders appear at the rounded neckline, as sleevelets, and around the skirt hem. Button back with handmade button holes. Circa 1900. $300/400

253. Blue and White Checkered Cotton Dress with Unusual Bodice Lacing
7" shoulder width. 18" waist. 17" overall length. Of a sturdy tightly-woven cotton in blue and white plaid, featuring a bodice that is styled like bébé stays, with brass-edged lacing grommets and laces, and a pleated skirt with constructed tuck on the skirt. Included is a white dimity blouse with lace-edged collar and puff sleeves, tucks at the front bodice. Circa 1890. $500/700

254. Red Cotton Dress with Linen Pinafore
5" shoulder width. 11" length pinafore. 14" length dress. A red cotton print dress with polka dot designs, printed border at skirt, and puff sleeves with bands, is protected by a fine linen pinafore with handmade embroidery at the neck and sleeves, red silk bows at the shoulders and a tie at the back. Circa 1890. $400/500

255. Navy Blue Polka Dot Dress with Pinafore

6" shoulders. 18" overall length. A navy blue cotton dress with white polka dots has a set-in yoke with gathers below and a ruffle at skirt edge. The sleeves and neckline are edged with dainty tatting, and there is blue and white striped muslin pinafore. Circa 1890. $300/500

256. Blue and White Checkered Cotton Pinafore Dress, Size 12

6" shoulder width. 17" overall length. A tiny and white checkered gingham creates a pinafore dress with fitted yoke edged by self-cording and embroidered collar, the yoke with alternating tucks and embroidered bands, above gathered full skirt, with attached ties at the waist, and having very full long sleeves with cuffs. The dress has original "12" label at the back, corresponding to size 12 Bébé Jumeau. Circa 1900. $300/400

257. Red Cotton Checkered Dress with "Pup and Chick" Borders

5" shoulder width. 14" overall length. A sturdy cotton twill pinafore dress with red checkered pattern has box-pleats down the entire front and back, square-cut neckline, very full long sleeves with cuffs, and back ties. The dress has red cotton border printed with a whimsical design of pups and chicks that is repeated at the neckline, cuffs and waistband, while a red and white checkered border is at the hem. Circa 1910. $400/500

258. Red Striped Cotton Dress with Cut-Work Detachable Bodice

8" shoulder width. 19" overall length. Red cotton dress with white pinstripes has stitched-down tucks at the yoke, very full pouf sleeves and constructed tucks at the lower skirt. A detachable bodice and collar is of exquisite cut-work with red embroidery and features a dainty scallop-edge rolled collar. Circa 1900. $300/500

259. Blue Flowered Chemise Dress for Bébé Jumeau
5" shoulder width. 14" length. The creamy muslin dress is printed with delicate blue flowers and features a narrow-pleated yoke with wide bretelles, puff sleeves, box-pleated dress front and ruffled hem. The neck and sleeves are trimmed with lace and blue silk ribbon. Circa 1895. $500/700

260. Blue Flowered Muslin Chemise Dress for Bébé Jumeau
4" shoulder width. 11" l. Creamy muslin dress with printed blue flower sprigs has a narrowly pleated yoke with wide pleated collar and bretelles, puff sleeves and box-pleated dress front captured with a detachable sash, ruffled hem. The neckline, collar, yoke, sleeves, and sash are trimmed with fine lace and pale blue ribbon. Signature dress for Bébé Jumeau from 1892 forward. Circa 1895. $500/700

261. Tan Leather Ankle Boots, Size 13
4 1/4". The tan leather boots with curved tops have three pairs of lacing grommets, original laces, and overcast stitching. Marked 13. Circa 1895. $200/300

262. BLACK LEATHER SHOES FOR BÉBÉ JUMEAU, SIZE 14
4 1/2"l. Of black leather with brown overcast stitching, the shoes have ankle straps with brown silk bows, and brown silk bow trim. Marked "Paris Depose 14" with bee symbol. Circa 1892. $200/300

263. BLACK LEATHER SHOES FOR BÉBÉ JUMEAU, SIZE 12
4 1/4"l. Of black leather with brown overcast stitching, brown silk bows, gold button on ankle straps, marked "Paris Depose 12" with bee symbol. Circa 1892. $200/300

264. RED FLOWERED CHEMISE FOR BÉBÉ JUMEAU WITH WAIST BANNER
5" shoulder width. 16" l. Creamy muslin dress is printed with red sprigs of flowers, and features a narrow-pleated yoke with lace edging that matches the lace around the neckline and puff sleeves. The dress front is box-pleated and captured under a detachable sash with a red silk label that is gilt-lettered Bébé Jumeau. There are additional ruffles and lace at the hem. Circa 1895. $600/900

265. BLUE FLOWERED MUSLIN CHEMISE DRESS FOR BÉBÉ JUMEAU
6 1/2" shoulder width. 19" overall length. The creamy muslin chemise dress is printed with sprigs of blue flowers, and has a fluted yoke and bretelles edged with lace that is repeated at the neckline. Below the yoke, the dress is box-pleated and a row of ruffles encircles the hem. There are very full sleeves with lace and blue ribbon edging that is repeated on the detachable sash with original gilt-lettered red Bébé Jumeau label. Circa 1895. $700/900

267. Blue Cotton Striped Dress

4" shoulder width. 11" overall. The cotton dress in a pretty pale blue and white stripe with darker blue pinstripe has a fitted yoke with lace and handmade zig-zag stitching that matches the trim on the neckline and gathered cuffs of the long sleeves, and having a full skirt. The trim extends around the back and has three pearl buttons with loop closure. Circa 1890. $200/250

266. White Cotton Pinafore with Blue Print

3" shoulder width. 10" overall length. The delicate white cotton is printed with a blue abstract design has square-cut neckline, very full puff sleeves with wide muslin and lace ruffle, and two pockets. Circa 1890. $200/250

268. Blue and White Striped Striped Two-Piece Dress with Brooch

4" shoulder width. 11" overall length. Blue and white variant stripes with interwoven raised dots comprising a blouse with dart-shaped waist, puff sleeves, and separate flared and pleated skirt. The dress has a separate collar with a little brooch pin. Circa 1900. $200/250

269. Blue and White Checkered Dress with Pinafore

3" shoulder width. 8" overall length. A blue and white checkered dress with simple gathered style is covered by a white cotton pinafore with scalloped-edge sleevelets and neckline, and having three rows of tucks around the hemline. There is a little brooch at the throat. Circa 1900. $200/300

270. Pale Blue Cotton Dress with Embroidery Panels

9" shoulder width. 19" overall length. The pale blue cotton dress with square-cut neckline has short puffed sleeves, dropped waist, front and back bodice with alternate bands of blue cotton and broderie anglaise, pleated blue skirt. The dress is further decorated with embroidered yoke, sleeve cuffs, and skirt hem. Circa 1890. $300/400

271. White Cotton Pinafore with Bertha Collar in Presentation Box

5" shoulder width. 11" overall length. The fine polished cotton pinafore with embossed texture features a wide ruffled Bertha collar with cut-work detail, gathered skirt with three tucks at the bottom. The pinafore is presented in a beautiful box with lithograph of young child. Circa 1890. $200/500

272. Two Pretty Silk and Cotton Dresses
8" and 10" shoulder width. Originally child costumes, but suitable for dressing larger dolls, each dress, one of cotton and one of ivory lace, is richly ornamented with lace, embroidery and other details. Circa 1900. $300/400

273. White Pressed Felt Flannel Bonnet in Unusual Shape
3" inside head width. 7" brim width. The pressed white wool flannel bonnet is designed to perch on the back of the head, framing the face. It has a wide half-moon brim that is decorated with blue bows and streamers on the inside and white boa draped georgette on the outside. The round cardboard frame and unusual shape suggests that the bonnet may have begun as a candy container. Circa 1890. $300/400

274. Woven Aqua Straw "Bird's Nest" Bonnet
The woven hat of curly and loosely woven aqua-dyed straw has a nest-like concave top and is decorated with silk flowers and leaves in a fanciful manner. There is some fragility to the hat. Circa 1895. $200/300

275. White Dotted Swiss Dress and Aqua Straw Bonnet
5" shoulder width. 11" waist. 15" overall length. 3" inside head width. A delicate dotted Swiss fabric comprises the sweet dress with fitted yoke edged with ruffles, blouson bodice, set-in waist, gathered skirt with tucks and ruffled hem, full sleeves with lace edging. Along with curly woven straw dyed aqua with upturned back brim and aqua silk satin bands and bows. Circa 1890. $400/600

276. White Dotted Swiss Dress with Splendid Silk and Lace Bonnet
5" shoulder width. 14" overall length. 4" inside head width. The delicate white cotton dress of dotted Swiss weaving features a fitted lace yoke, above blouson bodice, with cartridge pleated skirt, full long sleeves with lace edging. The dress is trimmed with lace bretelles and collar. Included is an ivory silk bonnet with dot-woven tulle overlay, ribbon loop edging, and a bouquet of ribbons and lace at the crown. Circa 1900. $500/800

277. Set of Fine Lingerie for Lady Doll

10" waist. 8" shoulder width. Designed for lady doll about 24". Of very fine muslin with richly detailed embroidery, laces, trim and rose silk ribbons, the set comprises night shift, petticoat, chemisette, pantalets, and drawers. Circa 1895. $300/500

278. Fifteen Bébé Stays and Corsets

Of various sizes and styles, the lot comprises a large assortment in delicate colors, with lace and button details, many with bone construction. Circa 1890. $500/700

279. Two Pairs of Shoes for Bébé Jumeau, E.J. Model
Each is soft black kidskin with brown overcast stitching, button closure on ankle straps and silk rosettes. Including 3" pair marked "E.J. Depose 10", and 2 1/4" pair marked "E.J. Depose 7". Circa 1884. $500/800

280. Three Pairs of Shoes for Bébés Jumeau
Each is black leather with brown overcast stitching, brown silk bows, and ankle straps, comprising 2 3/4" marked "Paris Depose 8" with bee symbol; 3 1/4" marked "Paris Depose 10" with bee symbol; and 3" marked "Bébé Jumeau Depose". Circa 1890 $400/600

281. Three Pairs of Doll Shoes
Comprising 3 1/4" pair of magenta silk with pom-pom trim and silk button closure, marked "Made in Germany" and "10"; 3" pair of rose twill with silver buckles and matching socks, marked "8"; and 2" cream kidskin with very fancy ankle straps marked "Modes de Paris". Circa 1900. $300/400

282. Five Pairs of Cotton Knit Socks
1" - 4" soles. Of finely woven cotton in a variety of weaves and colors, including sand, rose, tan and blue. Circa 1895. $100/200

283. Two Pairs of Shoes for Bébés Jumeau
Comprising 1 3/4" cream kidskin with overcast stitching and ankle straps marked "Paris Depose 2" and bee symbol; and 2" rose twill marked "Paris Depose 3" and bee symbol. Circa 1895. $300/500

284. Pair of French Pink Rayon Carnival Costumes with Amusing Decorations

9" shoulder width. 22" overall length. Of vibrant pink rayon, the clown-style costumes, created for child wear, are decorated with applique astrological emblems including rhinestone-studded sun, moon slice, and such. With black velvet pom-pom decorations. The matching pair of costumes are presented in their original packing from Aux Trois Quartiers Paris department store with invoice dated 1938. $500/800

285. Fine Traditional Costume with Black Velvet Embroidered Bodice
5" shoulder width. 10" waist. 13" overall length. Featuring a black velvet bodice with coat sleeves gathered at the shoulders and embroidered with flowers and leaves, maroon wool pleated skirt with blue border, silk brocade apron, floral-printed challis fichu with fringe, and a superbly embroidered and beaded vest and cuffs. Circa 1890. $600/900

287. Blue Flannel Wool Middy Jacket
Of fine quality wool, the classic middy style jacket has gold piping at the lapel edge and back collar, inset V-shaped panel with embroidered anchor, coat sleeves with gathering at the shoulders and set-in cuffs, and two rows of tiny decorative brass buttons. Circa 1900. $200/300

286. Patterned Blue Cotton Mariner Suit with Brass Anchors
5" shoulder width. 11" overall length. A midnight-navy-blue cotton two piece ensemble features a sleeveless dress with set-in but relaxed waist, pleated skirt, and separate middy jacket with small lapels decorated with brass anchors, yellow tie, and coat sleeves with gathering at the shoulders. Circa 1890. $300/500

288. Black Wool Flannel Middy Jacket
6" shoulder width. 6" length. A fine flannel wool classic middy jacket in an unusual black collar is trimmed with three narrow stripes on the lapel that continue to back collar, and long sleeves with constructed cuffs having striped trim. Along with a black silk tie. Circa 1900. $200/400

289. Navy Blue Cotton Serge Dress with Mariner Style Trim

5" shoulder width. 15" overall length. Of thickly woven cotton serge in a rich navy blue color, the dress features a full gathered skirt below the fitted high bodice. There is a set-in panel of cream wool at the yoke bordered by three rows of gold and cream braid; the gold braid is repeated on the constructed cuffs of the long sleeves which gain their fullness by shirring at the shoulder edge. The front bodice is repeated by the back. Circa 1900. $200/300

290. Textured Serge Sailor Suit with Dress and Jacket

5" shoulder width. 13" overall length. Of a navy blue/black rich color enhanced by textured fabric design, the set features a sleeveless dress with relaxed set-in waist above a wide pleated skirt, with embroidered anchor on the bodice. The dart-shaped jacket has wide self-lapels under a detachable cream ribbed collar with stitched stripes, narrow sleeves, and small decorative brass buttons. Circa 1890. $500/700

291. Navy Blue Wool Sailor Cap "Baby"

5" inside head width. The wool flannel sailor cap has a firm brim with silk grosgrain banding, and is decorated with metal gilt letters "Baby". Circa 1890. $200/400

292. Navy Blue Flannel Mariner Suit with Pale Blue Cotton Twill Bodice and Collar

5 1/2" shoulder width. 14" overall length. The two-piece ensemble features a sleeveless dress with blue cotton twill bodice decorated with three narrow white stripes at top and bottom, striped cotton bodice back (matching the jacket lining), and pleated skirt. The matching jacket has slightly flared side, very full sleeves with shoulder gathers and constructed tucks at the wrists, eight decorative brass buttons, and a pale blue over-sized middy collar with white stripes. Circa 1910. $500/700

293. Navy Blue Mariner Costume with White Collar

5" shoulder width. 13" overall length. A sleeveless dress with slightly-dropped waist has a pleated skirt and three narrow bands of decorative cording at the neckline and waist. Along with a matching jacket with elbow-length sleeves having generous gathers at the shoulders that are captured in constructed tucks at the sleeve edge, dart-shaped back and two pairs of tiny decorative brass buttons, with nifty white linen collar having inset cutwork band. Circa 1900. $400/500

294. Navy Blue Serge Sailor Suit with Cap, for Size 7 Bébé Jumeau

Of darkest navy blue linen-like serge, the suit comprises a sleeveless dress with cotton chambray bodice trimmed with white striping above a relaxed waist and pleated skirt. With middy jacket featuring full gathers at the shoulders and a detachable pale blue tie. There is an interesting variation of thick/thin striping that appears on the bodice, collar, tie and sleeves. Included is a blue woolen sailor cap with Au Bon Marche gold label in the lining. The size 7 label inside the jacket indicates its sizing for Bébé Jumeau 7. Circa 1900. $500/700

295. Navy Blue Twill Mariner Costume for Size 12 Bébé Jumeau

7" shoulder width. 16" over all length. Of sturdy navy blue twill, the ensemble comprises a sleeveless dress with blue chambray front panel, and relaxed waist above a pleated skirt. Along with a middy jacket featuring sleeves with full gathers at the shoulders, constructed cuffs of pale blue chambray with white stripes, and a matching chambray collar and tie. The "12" label is inside the jacket indicating its production for size 12 Bébé Jumeau. Circa 1900. $600/900

296. Blue and White Sailor Suit with Short Sleeves
5" shoulder width. 13" overall length. The summer sailor suit has a linen-like double-breasted middy blouse with wide navy blue collar trimmed with two bands of white piping, and blue turn-up cuffs with white piping. A pleated skirt with relaxed-fit waist band has all-around pleats and button-attachment to the blouse. Circa 1915. $300/500

297. Classic Mariner Suit with White Middy Blouse
5" shoulders. 12" overall length. A textured white middy blouse with button front that is captured by a set-in waist band, has 3/4 sleeves with navy blue cuffs decorated with three white narrow bands that match the navy blue middy collar, with blue silk tie. Along with sleeveless dress with navy blue pleated skirt having white stitching at the hem line. Circa 1910. $300/500

298. Maroon and Navy Blue Mariner Dress
4 1/2" shoulder width. 10" overall length. Having maroon flannel bodice with full sleeves that are gathered at the shoulders and having blue cuffs with white striping that match the unusual rounded collar that meets at the center front. The skirt is actually attached to the bodice although they appear as two pieces, and features neat pleat all-around with bone button trim. Circa 1915. $400/600

299. Two-Piece Mariner Summer Costume for Size 3 Bébé Jumeau
3 1/2" shoulder width. 10" overall length. The short-sleeved middy blouse of fine white flannel has a black linen-like middy collar and sleeve bands on the wide sleeves, and is trimmed with double rows of white braid. The blouse is button-attached to a black pleated skirt. There is a size "3" label inside the blouse indicating Bébé Jumeau or SFBJ size 3. Circa 1915. $300/500

300. Blue and White Woolen Two Piece Suit
5 1/2" shoulder width. 15" overall length. A tiny blue and white plaid wool forms a sleeveless dress with inset lace yoke, flat-front, and pleated side and back skirt. There is a matching jacket with curved front opening edged with woven buttons, and stitched-down lappets at the front and back. The long coat sleeves are gathered at the shoulders. Circa 1900. $300/500

301. Cream Coat with Silk-Edged Collar and Straw Bonnet for Bébé Jumeau, Size 6.

5" shoulder width. 11" overall length. Of fine ribbed fabric in a rich cream color, the coat has wide pleats that fall from a fitted yoke that is hidden beneath a very large collar. The lined coat has very full long sleeves with cuffs. The collar is decorated with two rows of applique braid and edged with a border of narrow-pleated ivory silk. Along with a bee-hive bonnet of woven straw with grosgrain edging and band, stamped "6" inside the hat. Circa 1895. $400/600

302. Brown Wool Trousers with Original Maker's Label

9" waist. 9" length. The brown woolen men's trousers with constructed pockets, cuffs and belt loops have an original label, "Dutchess Trousers, 10 cents a button, $1 a rip. Warranty. You may wear a pair for two months. If a button comes off, we will pay you 10 cents. If they rip we will pay you $1 or give you a new pair" suggesting the miniature trousers were a promotional stunt with a practical pleasure for young doll dressers. Circa 1900. $300/400

303. Taupe Wool Flannel Capelet Coat

5 1/2" shoulder width. 13" overall length. Of a very fine quality wool flannel, the taupe-colored coat has flared sides with overcast stitching in the manner of a quality tailor. Wide coat sleeves are curved at the wrists, and the 8"l. cape has dart-shaping at the shoulders and a graceful curved shape that corresponds exactly to the sleeve shape. The cape is s-curved at the back and the curve is mimicked by the five curved ribbon stripes that extend around the entire collar, and along the sleeves. The fine fabric and workmanship suggest production by a fine tailor. Circa 1890. $300/500

304. Amber Brown Woolen Skirt and Cape with Bonnet

6" shoulder width. 12" waist. 11" skirt length. A pretty amber brown wool forms a cape with rounded collar and a matching gored skirt, each trimmed with bands of brown silk ribbon. Along with a lace cap with brown grosgrain ribbons. There is some little moth damage on the wool. Circa 1890. $300/400

305. Brown Woolen Cape with Woven Straw Bonnet

50" (127 cm.) 6" shoulder width. 16" length. 4" inside head width. A brown wool flannel cape with fitted yoke that is hidden by the three-tiered graduated width collar, is beautifully flared and shaped. With a wide-brimmed woven straw bonnet with unusual brown painted finish, decorated with beautifully draped silk ribbons and floral and leaf monture. Circa 1900. $300/400

306. Plaid Silk and Cashmere Dress with Matching Jacket
4" shoulder width. 16" overall length. Beneath a waist-length jacket of plaid silk and cashmere with silk ruffled-edge wide collar and narrow fitted sleeves, is a matching sleeveless dress whose bronze-silk bodice has faux-tucks and a center rosw of tiny gilt buttons and having pleated skirt. Circa 1890. $200/300

307. Brown Woolen Lady's Fitted Jacket
6" shoulder width. 10" waist. 11" overall length. The thickly woven brown fitted coat has rounded collar, coat sleeves, shaped waist, pockets, handmade buttons holes, and a beautifully dart-shaped fitted back. Circa 1910. $300/500

308. Stylish Mink Stole with Collar
8" shoulder width. 7" length. The mink fur stole with dart-shaping to fit neatly over the shoulders is fully lined, and has a rounded collar. $100/300

309. Sage Green Woolen Lady's Suit
6" shoulder width. 10" waist. 22" overall length. Of a fine sage green wool/silk combination the lady's suit features the distinct shape of the Edwardian era, with exaggerated bosom and tiny waist. The suit has double collars with white stitching trim that is repeated on the sleeves and skirt, green velvet bodice insert, long fitted sleeves full at the shoulders and tapering to the wrists before flaring again, gored skirt. Circa 1910. $400/500

310. Lady's Two Piece Taupe Suit with Braid Trim
6" shoulder width. 10" waist. 22" overall length. Of a very fine taupe wool the ensemble features a fitted jacket with defined bosom and waist, long coat sleeves with gore detail at the shoulders, and generous trim of brown braid which runs down the length of the bodice and also serves as button loops. The gored skirt has pleats at the bottom edge, and there is beautifully accomplished rows of stitching on the jacket and following the seams of the skirt. Circa 1912. $500/700

113

311. Lady's Two-Piece Golden Ensemble from the Edwardian Era

6" shoulder width. 10" waist. 23" overall length. A two-piece ensemble with matching hat features a fitted jacket with velvet placket, dart-shaping, gigot sleeves with constructed velvet cuffs, and a nicely designed skirt with velvet front panels that sweep to the side and form a back lower skirt, having embroidered emblems, and golden tan wool/silk back. There is "jeweled" bead trim at the neckline and cuffs. Circa 1912. $300/500

312. Theatrical Costume in the 19th Century Style, Early 20th Century, on Stockman Mannequin

6" shoulder width. 13" waist. 25" overall length. A two-piece gown of changeable silk features a rounded neckline with embroidered tulle ruffle, dart-shaped bodice with bone construction, very pouf sleeves with lace ruffle, and a gathered long skirt. Along with original rayon petticoat with lace edging, and presented on original linen-covered wooden mannequin with wooden pedestal, and marked by mannequin maker, Stockman of Paris. The costume, in the 18th century style, appears to be a theatrical miniature costume, early 20th century. $500/800

313. White Cotton Lady's Gown in the Edwardian Style

5" shoulder width. 11" waist. 15" overall length. White cotton one-piece gown with scalloped-edge bodice has a ruffled edge of lace at the yoke and descending down the very full bodice, having full sleeves with lace edging, set-in waistband, gored skirt with three layers of lace at the hemline. Circa 1915. $300/500

314. Rose Cotton Lady's Two-Piece Costume

5" shoulder width. 11" waist. 18" overall length. Of tightly woven rose cotton, the two-piece ensemble features a dart-shaped bodice with fitted yoke, lace edging, gigot-style sleeves, and having a skirt that is flat-paneled at the front and gathered at the back. Circa 1910. $300/500

315. White Fur Coat with Matching Muff

6" shoulder width. 10" l. The white fur coat with wide collar and sleeves features decorative fox tails at both front and back, and has a matching muff with silk lining and cord handle. Circa 1910. $300/400

316. Mohair Coat with Cashmere Collar and Muff

Of very silky long curly mohair, the coat has a rounded wool collar with soutache embroidered details, is fully lined and includes a mohair muff decorated with white berries and leaves. Circa 1900. $400/600

317. White Fur Collar and Muff with Blue Silk Lining

4" l. muff. A white fur collar or stole is decorated with fox tails and has a blue silk lining. Along with a matching muff with blue silk lining and blue cord. Circa 1900. $200/300

318. Pale Green Fleecy Coat, Muff and Cloche with Fur Trim

6" shoulders. 11" length. Of pale apple green fleecy flannel, the three-piece ensemble comprises a coat, muff with cord handle, and cloche-style hat, each trimmed with white fur. Circa 1930. $300/400

319. Purple and Silk Velvet Coat with Embroidered Lapels and Cap

8" shoulder width. 14" length. Rich purple velvet coat in the 1920s style has ivory plush lapels and cuffs that are enhanced with mauve floral embroidery, purple silk lining. Along with mohair cap with purple silk banding, and lining. Circa 1920s. $300/500

320. BLACK WOOLEN COAT FOR BÉBÉ JUMEAU, SIZE 6
5" shoulder width. 10" length. Of very fine silky wool, the short black jacket coat has brass buttons with anchor designs, blue cotton lining, collar, coat sleeves. Original size tag "6" for Bébé Jumeau appears at the back inside collar. Circa 1910. $200/300

321. PLAID WOOLEN HOODED JACKET FOR BÉBÉ JUMEAU, SIZE 10
6 1/2" shoulder width. 13" overall length. Plaid silky wool fabric in shades of green, black and red form a nicely fitted jacket with coat sleeves that are slightly gathered at the shoulders, and having gathered hood with red silk lining. The jacket has cotton lining and brass buttons with raised anchor design, and has its original size label "10" indicating its production for Bébé Jumeau, size 10. Circa 1900. $300/400

322. SLATE GREY WOOLEN GREAT-COAT FOR BÉBÉ JUMEAU, SIZE 7

4" shoulder width. 10" length. The fine slate-grey woolen great-coat has slightly dropped-waist, double-breasted styling, brass buttons with anchor design, one row of button holes, stand-up collar with brass anchors at the tips, gathered skirt, coat sleeves with stitched outline of cuffs, and detachable belt. The original size label "7" is stitched at the back collar, indicating production for Bébé Jumeau, size 7. Circa 1890. $300/400

323. BLUE VELVET COAT WITH ANCHOR BUTTONS FOR BÉBÉ JUMEAU, SIZE 9

6" shoulder width. 12" overall length. A rich royal blue velvet forms a coat with slightly flared sides, sateen lining, and black trim at the middy-style collar and cuffs. The coat has brass buttons with raised design of anchors. An original size tag "9" appears on the inside back, indicating its original production for Bébé Jumeau, size 9. $300/400

324. BLUE VELVET COAT FOR BÉBÉ JUMEAU, SIZE 8

5" shoulder width. 11" length. Of lustrous midnight-blue velvet, the coat features middy-like collar that extends low at the back. There are three brass buttons with raised anchor designs, and an applique of black silk braid. The size number "8" appears at the inside neck, indicating its production for size 8 Bébé Jumeau. Circa 1900. $300/400

325. Felt Costume with Applique Designs in Presentation Box

A creamy felt coat and cloche are each decorated with bands of pale blue felt and has scalloped-edging with colorful polka dots and overlapping leaves. There is a little brass-plated piglet brooch attached, and the set is presented in a colorful box with an image of a child playing with her dolls. 5" shoulder width. 10" length. Circa 1930. $300/400